©2015: L. Larry Liu (self-published)
CreateSpace
Charleston, SC, US
ISBN-13:978-1502868855
ISBN-10:1502868857
The Austerity Trap: Economic and Social Consequences of Fiscal Consolidation in Europe/ L. Larry Liu
1.Business and Economics-Public Finance. 2.Political Institutions and Public Administrations (Europe)

The Austerity Trap: Economic and Social Consequences of Fiscal Consolidation in Europe

By L. Larry Liu

"Insanity is repeating the same mistakes and expecting different results."
World Service Conference of Narcotics Anonymous (1981), p.11

"Austerity doesn't work... It has instead brought us class politics, riots, political instability, more rather than less debt, assassinations and war."
Mark Blyth, *Austerity: The History of a Dangerous Idea* (2013), p.229

Table of Content

Abstract...6
Chapter 1: Introduction...7
Chapter 2: Spain...10
Chapter 3: Portugal...16
Chapter 4: Italy...23
Chapter 5: Cyprus...31
Chapter 6: Ireland...37
Chapter 7: United Kingdom...45
Chapter 8: Latvia...55
Chapter 9: The Argument on Austerity...62
Chapter 10: The Eurozone Crisis and the Power of Financiers and Germany...70
Chapter 11: The Solution to the Crisis and the Alternatives to Austerity...78
Chapter 12: Conclusion...89
Postscript...90
References...92
Appendix...123
Index...128
About the Author...139

The Austerity Trap: Economic and Social Consequences of Fiscal Consolidation in Europe

Abstract

In the wake of the eurozone crisis, and the banking and economic crisis, many European countries have experienced an increase in the government debt load. The governments of Europe acting under the pressure of the troika, consisting of the European Commission, the European Central Bank and the IMF, have pledged to austerity policies in the hope that reducing government spending and raising taxes would alleviate the debt burden, and improve consumer and investor confidence and export, leading to the anticipated economic recovery.

This book studies the social and economic consequences of austerity policies in seven European countries (Spain, Portugal, Italy, Cyprus, Ireland, UK and Latvia), and argues that the austerity policies in Europe have deteriorated rather than improved the fate of the European economies; increased rather than decreased the national debt; and raised rather than alleviated social suffering through enormous cutbacks in the social welfare, health care and education systems; the lay-off of many public-sector workers; the increase of the unemployment rate; labor market reforms that made employment relationships more insecure and reduced wages; a deterioration in overall health; a rise in suicide and depression rates; and a rise in social unrest. The book also offers alternatives to the current impasse in the eurozone, including a cancellation of debts; a tax increase on the wealthy; a break-up of the eurozone followed by currency devaluation in the periphery; the increase in domestic consumption in the surplus countries, such as Germany, and a stimulus program for the periphery; and the creation of a EU fiscal union.

Chapter 1: Introduction

In Greece, the enormous austerity measures inflicted by the troika, consisting of the European Commission, the European Central Bank and the IMF, are weakening the economy and deteriorating the living standards of the people. Youth unemployment has now risen to 64.2%, the overall unemployment rate is about 27% (Georgiopoulos and Maltezou 2013). The government of Greece had passed an austerity budget in November of 2011 worth €13.5 billion in a two-year time frame, raising the retirement age from 65 to 67, while cutting pensions between 5% to 15%. Public-sector workers face one third in pay cuts, and have their bonuses scrapped. Labor laws have also seen changes. Redundancy notice periods were reduced, compensation for long-term employees was limited, and companies were permitted to force their employees to work longer (Labropoulou and Smith-Spark 2012). 15,000 public sector workers are being laid off until the end of 2014. Net monthly minimum wages were set at €490 for workers above the age of 25 and €427 for those below 25 (Keep Talking Greece 2013b). Real wages in Greece have decreased by 22% since 2009 (Janssen 2013). An emergency property tax, costing each household several hundreds of euros, is collected via the electricity bill. It had been implemented in 2011, and will continue in 2013 (Keep Talking Greece 2013a). The purpose of all this austerity for Greece is to qualify for a €31.5 billion foreign loan in order to continue paying its bills. An important portion of Greece's expenditures goes to debt service (19.8% as of 2011- Charalabidis 2011) instead of job creation and productive investments. Out of the €207 billion that have thus far transferred to Greece in loans, €160 billion went to benefit banks and capital owners (FAZ 2013).

The question arises whether the austerity measures are doing any good. The IMF, which admits having underestimated the impact of austerity on the Greek economy, calling it a notable failure (Irish Examiner 2013), has cut the growth outlook of the world economy from 3.5% from the January 2013 forecast to 3.3% in April. The United States will grow by 1.9% instead of the predicted 2.1%. The eurozone will shrink by 0.3% instead of by 0.1% (Thompson 2013). For Greece, the public debt still stands at 157% of GDP at the end of 2012, and remains higher than sustainable (IMF 2013). The human costs have also been enormous. About 20% of the Greeks live in poverty (Kouvoussis 2013). The suicide rates in the first four months of 2011 spiked by 40% from 2010 (Euro Health Net 2011). The 40% cuts in the national health budget since 2008 have thrown 35,000 doctors and nurses out of work, increased wait times and drug costs, increased infant mortality by 40%, doubled the increase in new HIV infections (due to an increase in intravenous drug use following cuts in needle-exchange programs), and increased the number of malaria cases (due to cuts in mosquito-spraying programs) (Stuckler and Basu 2013a).

Illustration 1: Austerity Measures and Impact on GDP

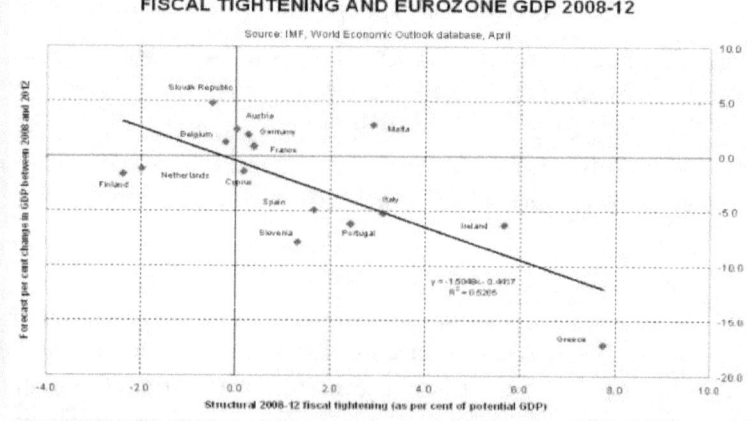

Austerity is a social and economic disaster (Arestis and Pelagidis 2010; Islam and Chowdhury 2010; Jayadev and Konczal 2010; Lapavitsas et al. 2010; Emmott 2012; Han 2012; McKee et al. 2012; Blyth 2013a; Collignon 2013; Skidelsky 2013; Stuckler and Basu 2013b). 17 European countries in 2010

have implemented €487 billion in austerity packages, which has led to a -2.7% GDP growth shrinkage in these countries (Theodoropoulou and Watt 2011, 12). Martin Wolf (2012) finds that 1% of GDP of fiscal tightening (i.e. austerity) yields in a contraction of GDP by 1.5% (cf. Illustration 1). But organizations like the IMF and the European Union argue that "structural reforms" are necessary in order to improve the long-term fiscal health of the country.[1] The IMF (2013), for example, demands that Greece should ease regulations in the labor market by easing the firing of workers, dismantling collective bargaining agreements, and reducing the minimum wage (p.15); it should, furthermore, improve tax collection (p.22) and privatize state assets (p.23). The rationale is that lower wage labor costs will improve the export economy while increasing the confidence of investors to make investments, which will improve the economy (e.g. IMF Survey Magazine 2013; OECD 2011, 136).

However, I will argue that austerity is a policy, which exacerbates the economic crisis rather than solve it. In order to examine this claim, I want to summarize the austerity policies that have been carried out in the European countries other than Greece, such as Spain, Portugal, Italy, Cyprus, Ireland, the United Kingdom, and Latvia to identify the social and economic consequences of austerity. Based on this empirical analysis, I will then present the arguments on behalf of austerity and debunk the claim that austerity is a viable solution to the economic challenges confronting Europe. I will then outline the challenge in the eurozone and theorize on the power of financiers and Germany, which are driving austerity in Europe. I will conclude with some notes on alternative solutions to the political and economic crisis in Europe. The appendix lists the eight countries' budget balance, debt-to-GDP ratio, GDP growth and unemployment rate between 2007-13, and the size of the austerity packages in different EU countries.

---

[1] Academic literature, especially from economists, also emphasizes the importance of "structural reforms" within the framework of political economy, e.g. Rodrik (1996); Bergeijk, van Sinderen and Vollaard (1999)

Chapter 2: Spain

Spain's economic development had been built on a housing bubble. Since Spain's property bubble burst in 2008, the economy quickly deteriorated, and the government bailed out the banks (Duthel 2010, 54-56). Many local savings banks, that had loaded up bad debts, were forced to merge. Bankia, a major bank, had reported a loss of $25.2 billion in 2012, and received $23.5 billion from the EU rescue fund (Chislett 2013, 178). The Spanish government was so overwhelmed by these huge bank debts that the EU passed a €100 billion aid package to help out Spanish banks.[2] The essential dilemma in Spain is that it suffered from a competitive disadvantage upon entering the eurozone, with its current account deficit rising to 10% of GDP in 2008 (Pettinger 2012). Due to a deteriorating economy, the government surplus of 1.9% of GDP in 2008 turned into a deficit of -9.4% in 2012 (cf. Illustration 2).[3] The relatively low government debt of 36.1% of GDP in 2008 turned into a high debt burden of 84.2% of GDP in 2013 (cf. Illustration 3).[4]

Illustration 2: Spain Government Budget Balance

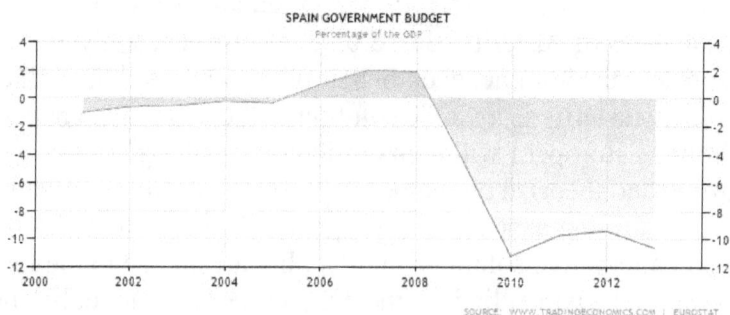

---

2 Wikimedia Foundation, "The Eurozone Debt Crisis."
3 Trading Economics, "Spain Government Budget."
   http://www.tradingeconomics.com/spain/government-budget
4 Trading Economics, "Spain Government Debt to GDP."
   http://www.tradingeconomics.com/spain/government-debt-to-gdp

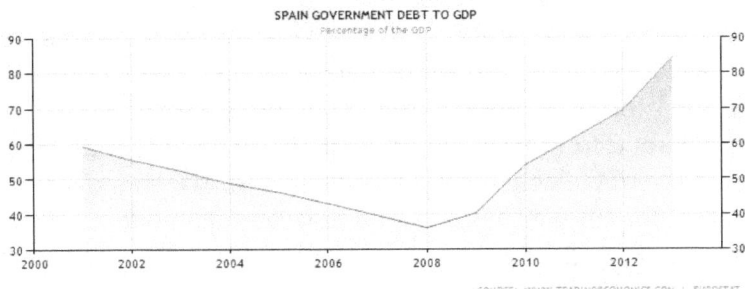

Illustration 3: Spain Government Debt-to-GDP Ratio

The government of Spain did not begin the austerity measures until 2010. In 2009, the socialist government under the leadership of Jose Luis Rodriguez Zapatero pushed for a stimulus program and supported automatic stabilizers such as unemployment insurance to help the unemployed to get by (Feigl 2012). But the financial markets punished the Spanish government in the spring of 2010 with higher interest rate surcharges (10 year government bond reached a peak of 7.5%, but not until July 2012[5]). European fiscal targets tightened, inducing the government to raise €11 billion in new taxes (Kyero 2009). In May 2010, the government passed another €15 billion austerity package. Civil servants' wages are to be cut by 5% per year (Dowsett 2010). Another austerity program passed parliament in December 2010, involving the sell-off of government stake in the national lottery, cutbacks in jobless benefits, tax cuts for small businesses and a hike in the tobacco tax (Clendenning 2010). This package involved a 7.9% cut in state-level spending, and a 16% cut in departmental spending (EWN Business 2011).

A conservative government under Mariano Rajoy was elected into office in 2011. The continuous increase of the unemployment rate and the shrinking economy made the government fail to reach the fiscal targets to lower the deficit and debt (Feigl 2012). The government continued with austerity. In January 2012, it

---

5 Trading Economics, "Spain Government Bond 10Y."
   http://www.tradingeconomics.com/spain/government-bond-yield

announced spending cuts of €8.9 billion, including a €1.6 billion reduction in public works projects. Income and capital taxes were raised (RTE News 2011b), while corporate taxes were reduced accounting for 70% of the drop in revenues (Gestha 2011, 5). A labor market reform that was passed in February 2012 saw a dismantling of collective bargaining rights for workers; more flexibility for employers to determine wages and hours; and less severance payments for workers who are laid off (Ministry of Economy and Competitiveness 2012).

In July 2012, another austerity package pledged to cut spending and raise taxes by €65 billion in a two-and-a-half-year time frame. The retirement age was increased from 65 to 67, wages for civil servants was cut further, state-owned companies were shut down, tax deductions for homeowners were scrapped, subsidies to political parties and labor unions were reduced by 20%, unemployment compensation was reduced to encourage people to find work (at a time when the unemployment rate was high) (Giles and Woolls 2012). The sales tax increased from 18 to 21% (Al Jazeera 2012). In September 2012, the government revealed a program to cut ministerial spending by 12%, freeze civil servant salaries, a 20% tax on lottery gains above €2,500 (BBC 2012a). In December 2012, the government passed a bill to permit the privatization of public hospitals in the hope to reduce spending (Rosales 2012). Education has been cut by 14% between 2012 and 2013, leading to a rise in tuition fees, larger class sizes and fewer grants for graduate studies (Al Jazeera 2013a). The student-to-teacher ratio will increase by 25%, teacher salaries were cut, university tuition fees were hiked by 66%, and scholarships were reduced by €50 million (Verger 2013).

Spain's budget projections still exceed the deficit target set by the European Union as the recession continues (Benoit 2012). When the unemployment rate jumped to 27.2% in April 2013, the government announced to ease the pressure through austerity by easing deficit targets to 6.3% of GDP, while allowing budget deficits to stay above 3% until 2016 (Moffett and Patnaude 2013). Nonetheless, austerity remains on the agenda. A report published by the Insituto de Estudios Fiscales called for a cut in pensions of 22-45% (Moral-Arce 2013, 24). In May 2013, the public works ministry planned to close 48 state-run rail routes and reduce services by 32% on the remaining routes, saving €86.5 billion per year. Fare prices were hiked by 3%. Energy subsidies for solar and wind power were cut by €4 billion, which will mean an increase in electricity prices for consumers. The government also cut €9 billion from local government administrations, leading in possible layoffs of local government workers. Care for disabled people was cut by €1 billion (Lopez 2013). Hospital privatizations are projected to cut spending by 20% (Press TV 2013a). In order to combat, the high unemployment rate, the Spanish central bank was calling for a suspension of the minimum wage in the hope to make Spain's products more competitive (Roman and Brat 2013). In June 2013, the government announced public-sector spending cuts, which will save the state €6.5 billion. 57 public entities are merged or shut down (Local 2013b).

The important question is what impacts these austerity measures had on the Spanish economy. While fiscal consolidation was in place, the economic growth rate turned from 2.5% in 2008, -3.5% in 2009, -1.4% in 2010, 0.5% in 2011, -0.7% in 2012 to -2% in 2013 (each for the first quarter; cf. Illustration 4). While the economy has seen some ups and downs, the unemployment rate has continuously increased, being raised from 8.6% in 2008, 13.91% in 2009, 18.83% in 2010, 20.33% in 2011, 22.85% in 2012 to 27.2 % as of April 2013 (cf. Illustration 5). Youth unemployment hit 57% as of May 2013 (Homs 2013). As a result of the labor market reforms, Spanish workers have lost wages (0.6% in the first quarter of 2013) (Tremlett 2013b). On the other hand, exports were increased, while imports decreased, leading to a smaller deficit in the current account. After peaking in 2008, reaching -10%, the current account deficit was reduced to -1.9%

in 2012.[6] But the apparently enhanced export competitiveness has not resulted in a lower unemployment rate which is continuing to increase, while the economy turning negative again starting in 2012 indicates that the austerity policies have depressing effects on the Spanish economy.

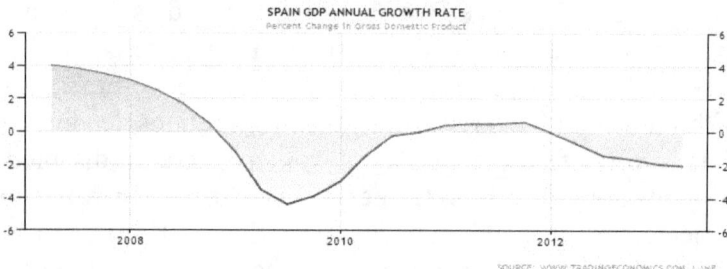
Illustration 4: Spain Annual GDP Growth Rate

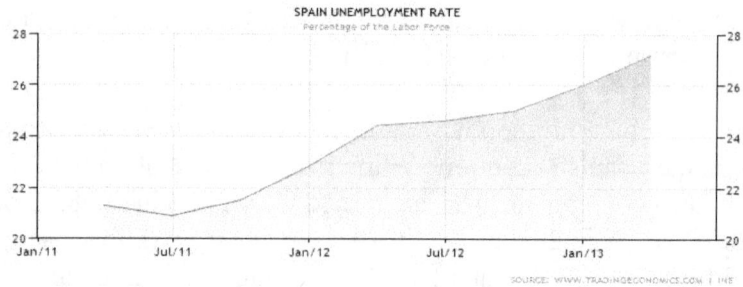
Illustration 5: Spain Unemployment Rate

Besides the economic consequences, the austerity policies have other social consequences. For example, cuts in the arts and theater programs have led to a 49.8% decline in the activity of cultural organizations (Woolfe 2013). 14% national budget cuts in health and social services in 2012 have led to greater demand for care among the elderly, disabled and mentally ill. Rising unemployment amid austerity also coincides with more suicides,

---

6   Trading Economics, "Spain Current Account to GDP."
    http://www.tradingeconomics.com/spain/current-account-to-gdp

depression and alcohol-related disorders. Suicides in Catalonia increased by 10% from 2010 to 2011 (Gallardo 2012). As a result of the austerity measures unofficial immigrants have been excluded from medical coverage, and patients have been forced to pay for extra services, such as drugs, prosthetics and ambulance treatments. The regional governments in Madrid and Catalonia have already implemented severe cuts in health spending that have led to the privatization of hospitals, longer waiting times, and fewer emergency services and surgical procedures (Kelland 2013; Legido-Quigley et al. 2013). 27% of the population are at risk of poverty or social exclusion in 2011 compared to 22.9% in 2008.[7] Several anti-austerity protests have rocked Spain (e.g. Day and Cobos 2012; Heckle 2012; Gates 2013), indicating greater social discontent.

---

7   Eurostat, "People at Risk of Poverty or Social Exclusion." http://epp.eurostat.ec.europa.eu/tgm/refreshTableAction.do;jsessionid=9ea7d07d30e7602b23e48da74ae1b4d1af719ab6d8d6.e34OaN8PchaTby0Lc3aNchuMc30Re0?tab=table&plugin=1&pcode=t2020_50&language=en

Chapter 3: Portugal

Portugal did not face the same housing bubble that Ireland and Spain went through. It suffered instead from a combination of low growth, an aging population, and low productivity (Blyth 2013a, 68; Pereira and Lains 2012). When the crisis in Greece set off in 2010, making many investors worried about the risk of holding Southern European debts, Portugal's 10-year bond interest increased from a low of about 4% in late 2009 to a high of about 17% in early 2012.[8] The government budget deficits as percentage of GDP increased from about 3.6% in late 2008 to 6.4% in late 2012 (cf. Illustration 6). The government debt-to-GDP ratio increased correspondingly from 71.7% in late 2008 to 123.6% of GDP in late 2012 (cf. Illustration 7).

Illustration 6: Portugal Government Debt-to-GDP Ratio

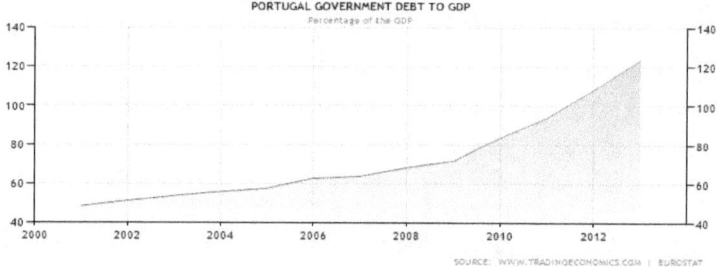

In May 2010, the government under Jose Socrates had reacted to the market pressures of greater bond yields and a budget deficit reaching 9.8% by passing an austerity program involving a 45% tax rate on incomes above €150,000 a year, and a 20% capital gains tax on stock market profits, while civil servant wages were capped and unemployment insurance limited (Khalip 2010). In October 2010, the Socrates government passed another austerity package to calm the markets and prevent a bailout, involving a 5% cut in public-sector pay, and an increase in sales taxes from 21% to 23% (Businessweek 2010), leading to huge labor strikes

---

8 As of June 2013, the 10-year government bond recovered to 6.5%. Trading Economics, "Portugal Government Bond 10Y." http://www.tradingeconomics.com/portugal/government-bond-yield

(Spiegel 2010). Portugal's government came under so much financial pressure, that it finally requested and received a €78 billion IMF-EU bailout package in May 2011. While the unemployment rate was increasing and the GDP was shrinking, the new government under Pedro Passos Coelho pledged to carry out an austerity program by raising taxes, cutting spending, freezing civil service salaries among low-income workers, and cutting civil service salaries among high-wage workers by 14.3%. The interest rate for the bailout was fixated at 5.1%, and in return Portugal pledged to austerity in order to reduce the budget deficit to 3% of GDP by 2013.[9]

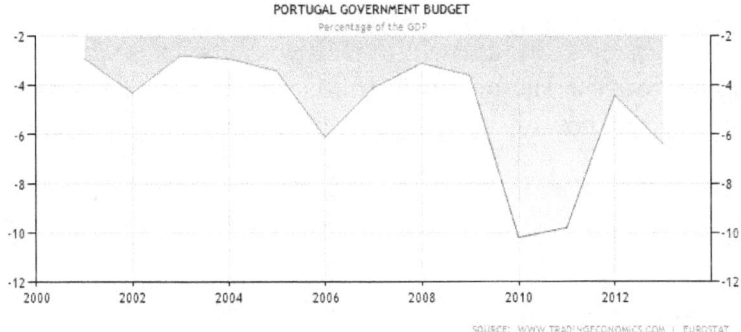

Illustration 7: Portugal Government Budget Balance

The fiscal target was met in 2011 with a 4.5% budget deficit due to a €6 billion one-off transfer of pension funds from banks into the state social security system (Kowsmann 2011). As of late-2012, however, the budget deficit increased to 6.4%, indicating the failure to meet the fiscal targets. As part of the bailout deal, Portugal also agreed to give up its shares in companies such as Galp Energia, EDP and Portugal Telecom, making the government thereby incapable to veto important decisions made by the companies (Khalip 2011). Privatizations thus far have been carried out in the energy sector, naval and defense construction, air transport, railroad, finance, communications, paper distribution, mining, media and water distribution. Home rentals

---
9 Wikimedia Foundation, "The Eurozone Debt Crisis."

and land use were deregulated, and mining concessions are negotiated with transnational corporations (Caldas 2012). Coelho pledged to downsize ministries and public sector agencies, while privatizing companies (Cala 2011).

In September 2011, the government announced to reduce 1,700 managerial posts from the state administration and 137 public companies (Taipei Times 2011). In October 2011, the government announced to scrap the 13th and 14th month salary payment for civil servants earning more than €1,000 a month. Private-sector workers were expected to work an additional half an hour per day, despite increasing unemployment. The sales tax increased further, while health and education budgets were slashed by about 10% each (RTE News 2011a; Rial 2011). Electricity taxes were raised from 6% to 23% (Hatton 2012). In March 2012, the government announced no new austerity measures (Almeida and Reis 2012).

But this promise was broken in November 2012 with the passage of a new austerity budget. While the economy was shrinking further, deteriorating the budget outlook, the government was essentially forced to further raise taxes to comply with the deficit targets. The measures involved an increase in the state income tax from 24.5% to 28.5%; a rise in the top tax rate from 46.5% to 48% plus a 2.5% solidarity tax; a lowering of the top income threshold from €153,300 to €80,000; a surcharge of 3.5% for 2013. The tax increases were equivalent to a month of workers' wages, and were intended to raise government revenues by 30%. Spending was reduced by €2.7 billion (BBC 2012b). 70% of the Portuguese public opposed this austerity budget (France24 2012). In order to avoid bankruptcy, the government resorted to another round of austerity measures in May 2013 by announcing to raise the retirement age to 66, set the public-sector work week to 40 hours and laid off 30,000 public-sector workers in order to save €4.8 billion in three years (Bridge 2013).

Since the beginning of austerity in 2010, the government has implemented a labor market reform in the hope of making the country more competitive. Unemployment compensation had been curtailed from a maximum of 38 weeks to 26 weeks; severance payments have been reduced from 30 days per every year worked to 20 days; firings have been eased; collective bargaining was dismantled; wage determination was transferred to firms; the minimum wage has been frozen since 2011; overtime pay was cut in half; annual leave entitlement was cut from 25 to 22 days a year; and four national holidays were suspended (Eurobank 2013). As of June 2013, the deficits have widened. The deficit of the central administration and the social security system increased from €1.72 billion in 2012 to €1.91 billion. In order to comply with the EU and IMF austerity guidelines, all ministries will be obliged to cut spending by 10% each. While projecting a deficit of 5.5% for 2013, the government pushed the 3% deficit target from 2013 to 2015 (Lima 2013).

Since Portugal has been so consistently following EU/IMF prescriptions it had been praised by EU commissioner Oli Rehn for "being on the right path"(Schultz 2012). The finance minister, Vitor Gaspar, called the austerity measures the "best path to reinvigorate growth" (Reuters 2012). But in July 2013, Gaspar changed his mind and resigned from his post, citing a "significant erosion in public support for the policies he believed were necessary to clean up Portuguese state finances", indicating that he regards the austerity policies as failure (BBC 2013b).

The consequences of austerity in Portugal have been devastating. Instead of reviving economic growth, the economy has been continuously shrinking following the heavy austerity that was inflicted. GDP growth changed from 0.9% in 2008, -4.1% in 2009, 1.7% in 2010, -0.4% in 2011, -2.3% in 2012 to -4% as of March 2013 (cf. Illustration 8). The unemployment rate has been continuously increasing since 2008. It increased from 7.6% in 2008, 8.9% in 2009, 10.6% in 2010, 12.4% in 2011,

14.9% in 2012 to 17.7% in March 2013 (cf. Illustration 9). 43% of youth below 25 years are unemployed (Tremlett 2013a). Labor wage costs have been reduced in part thanks to the labor market reforms. The steepest year-on-year decline in wages occurred in 2012 (9.6%).[10] Following the austerity policies, Portugal pulled back in imports and moderately increased exports. The current account deficit shrunk correspondingly from a high of -12.6% in 2008 to -3% in late-2012.[11] Similar to Spain, increased export competitiveness in Portugal has not contributed to a lower unemployment rate, which is continuing to increase even as social protections have been weakened.

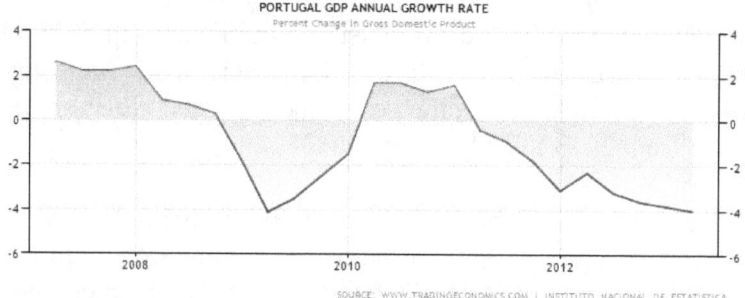

Illustration 8: Portugal Annual GDP Growth

---

10 Eurostat, "Labour Cost Index."
http://epp.eurostat.ec.europa.eu/portal/page/portal/labour_market/labour_costs/main_tables
11 Trading Economics, "Portugal Current Account to GDP."
http://www.tradingeconomics.com/portugal/current-account-to-gdp

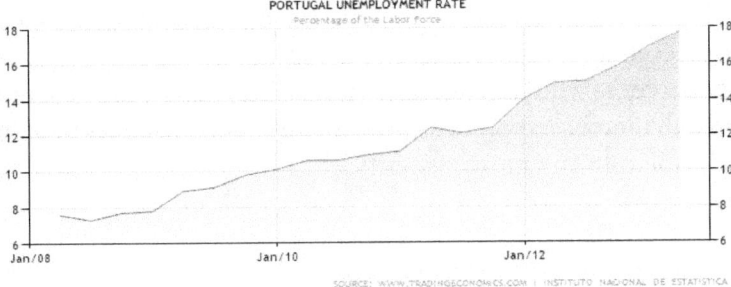

Illustration 9: Portugal Unemployment Rate

The social costs of austerity have similarly been enormous. The €1.5 billion in education cuts in 2012 have led to 25,000 teacher layoffs, salary freezes and 7.5% in salary cuts, 300 school closures, an increase in class sizes, and a reduction in social support for university students and university scholarships.[12] The health budget faced 20% cuts for 2013 (Paul Mitchell 2012). One hospital in the city of Evora, for example, has no doctors assigned in emergency rooms 40-50% of the time (Larouchepac 2013a). The government levied €20 in emergency room charges (Tremlett 2012). It also levied €20 in fees for a hospital visit, and €50 to get an x-ray. These were services that used to be for free, inducing Portuguese patients to skip medical treatment.

In the mean time, the need for health care is increasing. The death rate in the winter of 2012 has increased by 20% compared to previous years (Frayer 2012). Generally speaking, researchers suggest that increased unemployment and lower incomes are linked to more depression and long delays before seeking medical treatment (Karanikolos et al. 2013). People are also increasingly reporting trouble accessing food. The Portuguese Caritas reported a 46.5% increase in food aid requests from 2011 to 2012 (Hatton 2012).As a result of all these austerity measures, the people in Portugal have been in uproar, involving themselves in protests

---

12 Education in Crisis, "Portugal". http://educationincrisis.net/learn-more/country-profiles/europe/item/411-portugal

and strikes (e.g. France24 2011; Khalip 2012; BBC 2013a; Press TV 2013b) . Though the Portuguese have been relatively quiet and accepting of austerity during the initial period in comparison to the Greeks, who immediately went to the barricades (Khalip 2013), the increased protests indicate that the Portuguese can no longer tolerate any more austerity.

Chapter 4: Italy

Italy is a country that similar to Portugal grappled with low productivity, low growth and an aging population (Blyth 2013a, 68). Italy has kept the debt very low in the private sector, unlike Spain and Ireland, but the debt in the public sector has been very high, making Italy the third largest bond market in the world (with the eleventh-largest economy) (ibid.). Italy, very much unlike Spain, shunned foreign capital investments, and the state continued to protect inefficient companies such as the airline company Alitalia (Blyth and Hopkin 2010). Italy is also a country that has been suffering from a sharp north-south divide, in which the very wealthy northern part is subsidizing the poorer southern part (Mignone 2008, 181). On the other hand, the wealthy northern Italy has shielded the country somewhat from the enormous turmoil that afflicted the other Mediterranean countries. Since most Italians were not sufficiently taxed to pay for these across-country subsidies the debt burden had been increasing.

The Italian government had historically solved the accumulating debts via currency devaluation and inflation, but with the entry into the eurozone the devaluation stopped, and the debts were henceforth financed by low-interest borrowing. With the 2010 debt crisis unfolding in Greece, investors became more suspicious of the huge Italian debts, the low growth and low productivity, and interest rates spiked thereafter (Blyth 2013a). The high interest rates on the 10-year government bonds in Italy (reaching a peak of 14% in 1995) were moderated to between 4-5% since the late 1990s, and spiked to its recently highest level of 7% at the end of 2011. It has since come down to 4.5% in June 2013.[13] The government budget deficit increased from -1.5% in 2007 to -5.5% of GDP in 2009 during the recession, and has since been reduced to -3% as of late 2012 (cf. Illustration 10). The debt-to-GDP ratio has persistently increased from 103.6% in 2007 to 127% in late

---

13 Trading Economics, "Italy Government Bond 10Y."
http://www.tradingeconomics.com/italy/government-bond-yield

2012 (cf. Illustration 11).

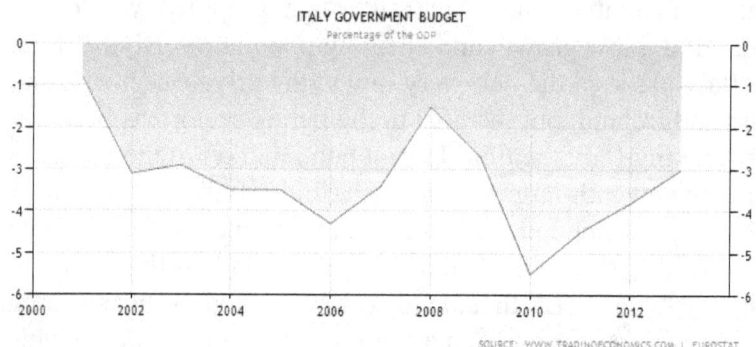
Illustration 10: Italy Government Budget Balance

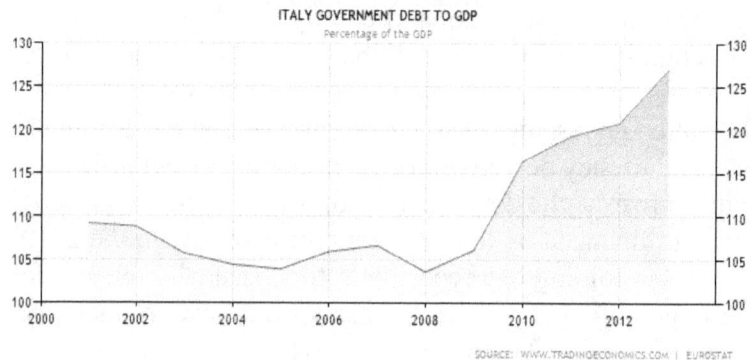
Illustration 11: Italy Government Debt-to-GDP Ratio

Following these fiscal developments, the Italian government led by Silvio Berlusconi began to implement austerity policies in May 2010. The government announced to reduce public sector pay, put a freeze on civil service recruitment, reduce public sector pensions and local government spending, and crack down on tax avoidance. The cuts comprise €24 billion, were equivalent to 1.6% of GDP, and were intended to reduce the deficit from 5.3%

to 3% in 2012 (BBC 2010b). The parliament raised the stakes by passing a $33 billion austerity package in July 2010 (New York Times 2010). The austerity plan also involved a delay in the retirement age by six months, a reduction in local government funding by €13 billion, and a reduction of ministerial spending by 10% in 2011 (Pietras 2009). €700 million were cut from the university budget, involving a reduction in the number of university lecturers and professors, and a transfer of university management into the hands of private investors (Arens 2010). Because the bond rating turned more unfavorable for Italy, Berlusconi's government pushed for another €48 billion austerity package in July 2011 involving spending cuts and tax increases to calm the financial markets (Channel4 2011). It sparked a major strike in September 2011 (Pisa and Pickup 2011).

As Italy's fiscal situation continued to deteriorate, Berlusconi wrote a 15-page letter of intent, laying out the proposals he wanted to implement, including a shrinking of government office space by 10%, a lowering of the university professor pension age from 70 to 68, and the introduction of a kindergarten tax (Speciale 2011). But when the investors pushed up the 10-year bond interest rate over 7%, Berlusconi was forced to resign in November 2011 after losing his parliamentary majority (Steinberg 2011a). He was replaced by Mario Monti, a former adviser to Goldman Sachs[14]

---

14 The reference to Goldman Sachs is relevant insofar as many other important European leaders, such as ECB chairman, Mario Draghi, or Greek prime minister, Lucas Papademos, were similarly high-ranking Goldman Sachs officials, indicating the influence and power of the bank over national economic policies, favoring austerity on the working population to guarantee state debt repayments to the banks. It is noteworthy as well that neither Monti nor Papademos were democratically elected. Goldman Sachs has notably covered up Greek debts with the help of a derivative deal (Balzli 2010). Greece itself owes huge amounts of money to banks. For example, €9 billion to Eurobank EFG (Greece), €8 billion to Piraeus Bank (Greece), €6.3 billion to FMS Wertmanagement (Germany), €6 billion to the Bank of Greece, and €5 billion to BNP Paribas (France) (Demonocracy.info, "Who Loaned Greece the Money?" http://demonocracy.info/infographics/eu/debt_greek/debt_greek.html).

and EU commissioner (Foley 2011). The appointed, i.e. unelected, technocratic government immediately went to work by announcing a new €30 billion austerity program titled "salvia italia" (save Italy), involving an increase of the retirement age from 58 to 66 by 2018; a cancellation of cost-of-living adjustments for pensions in 2012 and 2013; a reform in the pension system tying payouts to contributions rather than earnings[15]; an increase in the number of years worked in order to qualify for a full retirement from 35 to 42 years; and an increase in the value added tax from 21 to 23% (Steinberg 2011b). Other features involve cuts in education, health care, social welfare, deregulation of the labor market and the privatization of local and municipal services. In the mean time, large assets and estates, capital gains and high incomes remain untouched by the austerity program (Agnoletto 2012). Though the government has been increasing crackdowns against wealthy owners of Ferraris, generating $12 billion in tax revenues (Schifrin 2012).

The austerity showed its impact in April 2012, when Monti announced that the Italian economy shrunk by 1.2%, making the government unable to balance the budget by 2013 (Emsden 2012). In the same month, the government announced a labor market reform that eased the firing of workers; permits firms to cut hours of workers; eases the use of temporary contract workers; expands the hiring of contract workers; and expands the unemployment insurance coverage and limits it to 12 months for workers below the age of 55 and 18 months for those above it (Governo Italiono 2012). In July 2012, Monti announced another round of €26 billion cuts within a two-year period. A restructuring of regional governments will reduce the number of provinces from 107 to 59. Ten urban provinces will be turned into metropolitan areas to reduce costs. More than 3,000 organizations, administrative offices, and state enterprises will be cut (Arens 2012). Monti resigned from office in April 2013 after

---

15 The retirement changes decreases the pension amount from 70% of earnings to 56% (Carrera 2012).

parliamentary elections in February made his party rank fourth. The populist comedian, Beppe Grillo, channeled the anger and opposition of the Italians against the strict austerity policies, and received 26% of the national vote (Jones 2013).

Because Italy's budget deficit can be pushed down to 2.9% in 2013, with a projection to fall to 2.5% of GDP, even as the economy remains in a recession, and the debt-to-GDP ratio remains at 132%, the EU removed Italy from the 'crisis list' (Fox 2013). The new government under Enrico Letta has been calling for a small stimulus program. It will invest €3 billion in infrastructure projects and university subsidies to create 30,000 jobs (Stock Market Watch 2013). At a time when 3.27 million people are unemployed, this measure appears to be a drop in the bucket. Though Italy had been continuously in talks of receiving a EU bailout, it never received nor required any so far. Due to the size of its economy, and the enormous scale of the bailout amount required for it, Italy is thus far not expected to receive a bailout despite warnings that it will need them (Evans-Pritchard 2013).

The impacts of austerity policies on the economy and society have been severe. Italy's economy changed from 0.4% in 2008, -6.5% in 2009, 1% in 2010, 0.8% in 2011, -1.4% in 2012 to -2.4% in 2013 (cf. Illustration 12). The unemployment rate increased from 6.9% in 2008, 7.4% in 2009, 8.8% in 2010, 8.2% in 2011, 10.5% in 2012 to 12.2% in 2013 (cf. Illustration 13). It is noteworthy that the unemployment rate spiked after Mario Monti's austerity packages were passed. Labor costs have been somewhat moderated with the lowest year-on-year increase at the beginning of 2012 (0.1%), but have since picked up (2.5% in Q1 of 2013).[16] Throughout the eurozone crisis, the Italians have largely abstained from dramatically cutting the wage bill like in Spain or Portugal. On the other hand, the current account balance

---

16 Eurostat, "Labour Cost Index."
http://epp.eurostat.ec.europa.eu/portal/page/portal/labour_market/labour_costs/main_tables

has been consistently negative, because the deficit had been -3.3% of GDP in 2011, but was lowered to -0.7% in 2012.[17] An important characteristic of Italy is that though its debt-to-GDP ratio is significantly higher than Spain, Ireland or Portugal (though not Greece), it has maintained a lower unemployment rate than those countries, perhaps aided by the fact that wealthy northern Italy pulls up the average. The unemployment rate in the booming north-east Italy is 5%, whereas it is 14.1% in the islands of Sicily and Sardinia (Jung 2012). As of May 2013, Italy's youth unemployment rate is 40.5%, the highest since 1977 (CNBC 2013).

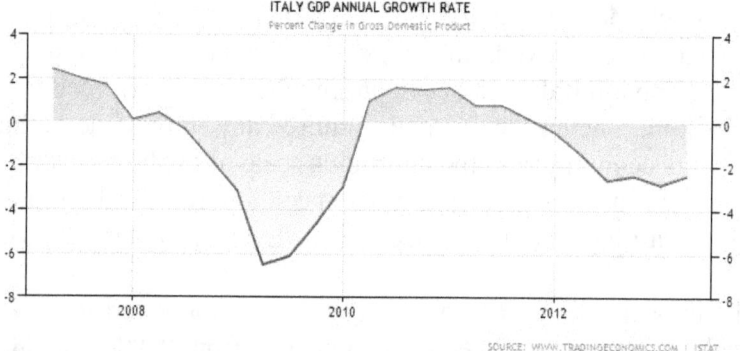

Illustration 12 Italy Annual GDP Growth Rate

The costs of austerity on society are similarly severe. The austerity policies have impacted health care spending. The central government has shifted more burden of health care spending to local governments, that often face large budget deficits and need to impose cuts (Belvis et al. 2012). Medical personnel decreased by 0.8% between 2009 and 2010 (Ragioneria Generale dello Stato 2010). As a result of cuts in public health services, the people have increased their private health care spending by 8%. The July 2012 austerity package is rolling over an additional €4 billion in health expenditures to the population going to accident,

---

17 Trading Economics, "Italy Current Account to GDP."
http://www.tradingeconomics.com/italy/current-account-to-gdp

emergency, diagnosis appointments and specialist appointments (Revolting Europe 2012). In a survey, 21% of Italians reported having decreased their health-related expenditures due to the financial crisis, and 10% postponed surgical treatment due to financial reasons (Belvis et al. 2012). Education has also fallen victim to austerity cuts. The government has reduced spending on public education by €8 billion between 2009 and 2012. It laid off 140,000 teachers and educational personnel since 2008. It merged 750 schools, and closed 450 mostly in the southern part of the country. Due to a €1 billion budget cut in higher education, the number of academic staff and researchers decreased from 64,000 to 54,000 since 2009.[18]

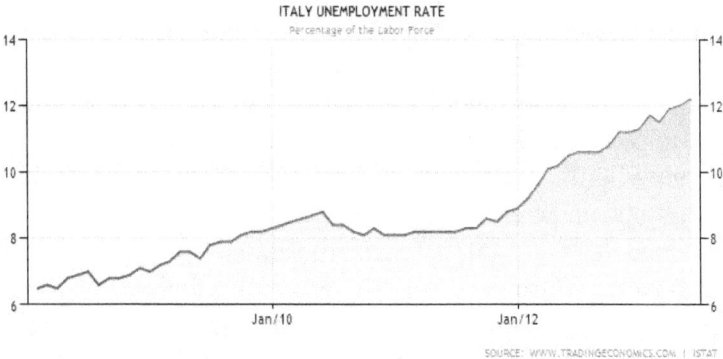

Illustration 13: Italy Unemployment Rate

Austerity also had an impact on the lifestyle of food-conscious Italians. People have been purchasing a record amount of flour, eggs, and butter in order to make pizza and bread at home rather than buying it ready-made from the store/restaurant, which is more expensive. A fresh loaf of bread costs about €5, while the ingredients to make the loaf cost around 80 cents. This has led many pastry shops to close for lack of business (Guttman 2013). Between 2009 and 2012, 33,000 businesses have failed. Business

---

18 Education in Crisis, "Italy." http://www.educationincrisis.net/learn-more/country-profiles/europe/item/413-italy

collapses have led to suicides of business owners (Squires 2012). Following the economic crisis suicide rates in the country have spiked by between 20 to 30% (Local 2013a). 59% of Italians are also re-cycling unfinished food rather than throwing it away (Ciancio 2012). Generally, the living costs for an average family have increased by €2,500 per year (Arens 2012). Due to the austerity measures, high petrol prices, and increased unemployment, Italians are increasingly switching from cars to bicycles (Kuo 2013).

Southern Italians, living in the mezzogiorno, particularly suffer from the austerity policies. Their unemployment rate is above national average. 150,000 jobs have been lost since 2007, and more than 1.35 million residents have migrated to the northern part of the country in search of work. In Basilicata and Calabria, hundreds of families are living in houses without electricity, children do not go to school, and people not able to afford food have resorted to raise animals themselves. 20% of Italian children are at risk of falling below the poverty line (Nadeau 2012). In Italy, 260,000 children below the age of 16 are forced to work (ANSAmed 2013). In 2011, 18.2% of Italians were considered at-risk of poverty (European Commission 2009). Italians have also reacted to the harsh austerity measures with numerous protests against the government policies (Squires 2010; Jones 2011; Euronews 2012; Al Jazeera 2013b).

Chapter 5: Cyprus

Cyprus, as a small island country with about 1 million residents, has based its economy on three foundations: shipping, tourism and banking (Stavrakis 2009). But the shipping and tourism industry was weakened with the onset of the recession in 2009, and the strongest viable sector was the banking system. Cyprus' secret was to offer an offshore tax haven for wealthy Russian oligarchs making up about one-third of total deposits. Foreign companies were offered a flat 10% tax rate to bank with Cyprus. Regulations on companies were very lax. Money kept on pouring in from abroad. 40% of the deposits in Cyprus are in excess of $650,000 (Gumbel 2013). By 2011, assets in the banking sector were seven times larger than the national GDP (Economist 2011). When the crisis hit it was eight times larger (Ghost Agenda 2013). The Cypriot economy seemed to be doing well, because it recovered from the slump in 2010 and 2011. But by mid-2011, economic growth turned negative as the banks were starting to face liquidity problems, and the government bond yield increased unfavorably. In order to prevent a EU bailout of its troubled banking sector, Cyprus has agreed to austerity measures in July 2011 (Parkinson 2011).

In August 2011, the parliament passed an austerity package, which included a 3% pay cut for civil servants, and an increase in the income and real estate tax (Kambas 2011). The top tax rate for incomes above €60,000 were raised from 30 to 35%; a 5-year income tax exemption on the first half of the income of foreign workers relocating to Cyprus was passed to lure foreign workers; dividend taxes were raised from 15 to 17% (Sovereign 2011). A second round of austerity measures was approved in December 2011, when the value added tax was raised from 15 to 17%, and the salary for both public and private sector workers were frozen for two years. Child and student benefit programs were cut (Cyprus Lawyer 2011). A 6% penalty was added to early retirements; permanent contributions for state employees toward retirement were levied; the 13th salary for state officials were scrapped, while they were lowered for lower-income civil servants; tobacco, alcohol and motor fuel taxes were raised; dividend taxes were raised by 1% and deposit taxes were raised by 0.015% (Euronomist 2012). This package induced a strike by civil servants (Financial Mirror 2011). The EU commissioner, Oli Rehn, praised the Cypriot government for all this austerity. "In a short period of time and in a decisive manner, Cyprus has adopted measures that are considered very satisfactory to help reduce the budget deficit", Rehn said (Cyprus Property News 2012).

All these austerity measures have neither helped Cyprus to consolidate its budget, nor to save its banks. What happened to the Cypriot banks was that they used a significant portion of their deposits to lend it to the Greek government. The trouble with the banks arrived in earnest when Greece in late-2011 negotiated a 74% haircut on the loans they owed to bondholders. The banks in Cyprus made an enormous loss, and required bailout assistance from their government, which was overwhelmed by the liabilities. With deposits eight times the size of the economy, the banks were too big to bail. The banks survived with the help of emergency liquidity assistance provided with the help of the ECB (Suoninen and Jones 2013). The government continued with austerity policies. In December 2012, it agreed to a further increase in the value added tax from 17 to 18%; property taxes are assessed at a higher value and are increased (Charalambous 2012). Public-sector workers' wages are to be cut by between 6.5 to 12.5%.[19] The government's wage bill should decline by 15%; social transfer payments were cut by 10%; and the number of public employees was targeted to be reduced by €250 per year for a total of €1250; overtime remuneration was cut by 20% (Euronomist 2012).

---

19 Famagusta Gazette, "Cyprus House Votes Twenty Three Austerity Bills into Law." Cyprus House votes twenty three austerity bills into law." http://famagusta-gazette.com/cyprus-house-votes-twenty-three-austerity-bills-into-law-p17475-69.htm

In March 2013, Cyprus requested financial assistance for the bailout from the EU and IMF. The EU agreed and, on March 16, granted Cyprus a €10 billion bailout deal under the condition that it would kick in €5.8 billion itself. In addition, €1.2 billion are to be raised in austerity measures (Ghost Agenda 2013). The government of Cyprus decided that it would do so by imposing a levy on bank deposits to raise the required amount. Depositors were slated to lose 6% of their deposits, and 10% for deposits above €100,000.

The lawmakers rejected the deal. In March 25, a new final deal was negotiated, in which Cyprus would still get the €10 billion EU-IMF bailout, while depositors below €100,000 had their deposits protected (Sansone 2013), but those above €100,000 faced levies of 20% (Tagaris and Kambas 2013). The Laiki bank, the second largest bank in Cyprus, is closed down, while the remaining assets are transferred to the Bank of Cyprus, the largest bank, to resurrect that bank. Depositors panicked and attempted to remove their deposits from the banks. To prevent massive capital flight (and an exacerbation of bank problems), the government imposed capital controls (Sansone 2013), allowing depositors to withdraw a maximum of €300 per day. A maximum of €2,000 in cash are permitted to be taken out of the country (Economist 2013). With an estimated 37% of the $68 billion deposits in Cypriot banks, much of which belonging to wealthy Russians, these Russians are slated to lose a large portion of their deposits. A spokesperson for Vladimir Putin called the deposit levy "unfair, unprofessional and dangerous" (Elyatt 2013). Russian oligarchs have already voiced their intent to shift their capital away from Cyprus and into Latvia (Ummelas 2013).

With the loss of their offshore tax haven status and the economic shock of the bank restructuring and austerity, Cyprus' economy is in freefall. Their growth rate has developed from 5% in 2008, 0.6% in 2009, -0.5% in 2010, 1.7% in 2011, -1.6% in 2012 to -4.3% in 2013 (cf. Illustration 14). The economy is expected to contract by 8.7% in 2013 (Parkin 2013). The positive government budget balance turned from 3.5% in 2007 to -6.3% in 2012 (cf. Illustration 15). The debt-to-GDP ratio is in an upward trajectory, increasing from a low of 48.9% in 2008 to 85.8% in 2012 (cf. Illustration 16). This ratio is expected to hit 109% of GDP in 2013.

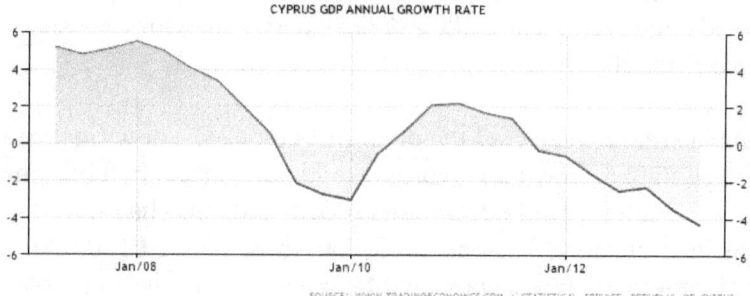
Illustration 14: Cyprus GDP Annual Growth Rate

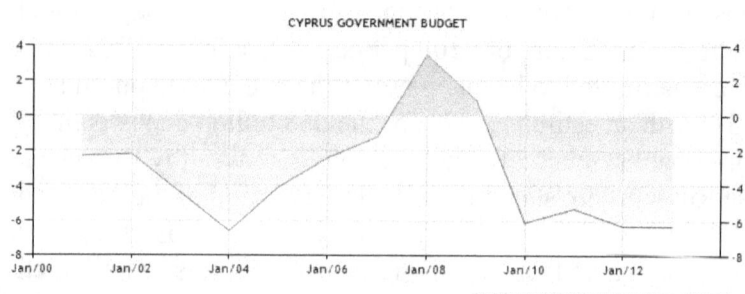
Illustration 15: Cyprus Government Budget Balance

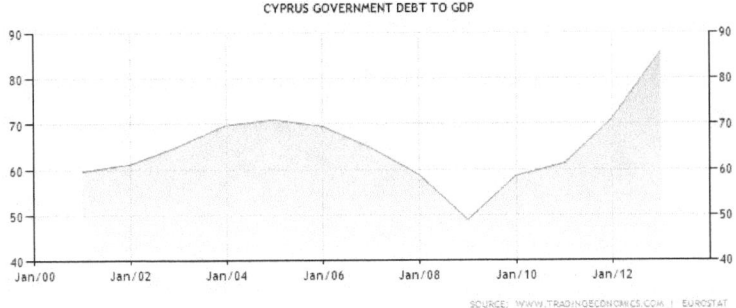

Illustration 16: Cyprus Government Debt-to-GDP Ratio

In the mean time, the banks are successfully deflating from 550% of GDP during the peak of the crisis to 350% of GDP. In order to follow the EU bailout guidelines, Cyprus has embarked on several further austerity policies as of April 2013. In order to reduce the deficit, it has sold 400 million in gold reserves, and announced the privatization of state assets worth €1.4 billion, including electricity, telecommunications and port authorities. 4,500 public-sector jobs are cut (total public-sector workforce is 70,000), and the remaining employees received pay cuts, the value-added tax, corporate tax, property tax, and excise tax will increase (Parkin 2013). Cost of living adjustment for workers are scrapped until 2016 (Stevens 2013). With an increasing amount of debt, and with a banking system in shambles, the austerity policies are adding more fuel to the fire. With the combination of the depositor tax, the capital controls, bank restructuring and austerity programs, the economy is declining rapidly (Persson 2013). The unemployment rate has consistently increased. It changed from 4% in April 2008, 4.7% in 2009, 6.8% in 2010, 6.9% in 2011, 10.3% in 2012, to 15.6% in 2013 (cf. Illustration 17). In the month of May 2013, unemployment rate had increased by 30% from May 2012.

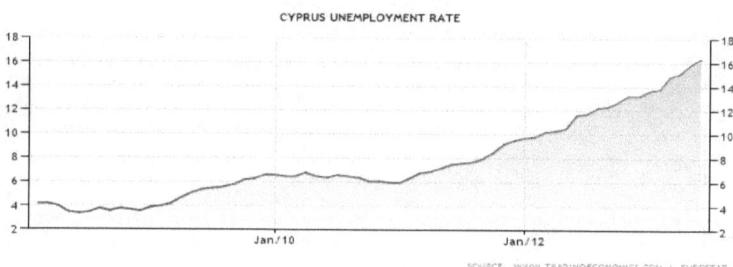

Illustration 17: Cyprus Unemployment Rate

In this time period, the retail industry shed 2,464 workers; the construction industry laid off 1,242 workers; civil servants were reduced by 1,391 (Georgiou and Tugwell 2013). The Bank of Cyprus alone has shed 1,000 employees (Psyllides 2013).

There have been other social consequences to austerity. The government has cut the higher education budget by 30.8% in 2012 (ESU 2013). Health care cuts have led to a cancellation of setting up a new regional ambulance station; funding for oncology radiotherapy centers has been frozen, threatening the lives of cancer patients (Larouchepac 2013b). The government has also scrapped plans to expand health care coverage to the whole population (Mladovsky et al. 2012, 19), and reduced the salary of health professionals (ibid. 23). Cypriots feeling betrayed by the EU (Alderman 2013) have staged protests against the bank restructuring and austerity plans (Davis 2013; Wearden 2013).

Chapter 6: Ireland

Ireland had long been a very poor country. In the mid-1990s, a huge amount of foreign direct investment entered the country, and it became an economic miracle, also known as the "Celtic Tiger". Ireland offered among the lowest corporate tax rates in Europe. The unemployment rate came down dramatically, and the economic growth rates and productivity growth rates picked up since that period. Starting with 2002, however, the boom relied increasingly on a growing housing market, similar to Spain. The state budget situation continued to improve, but mainly due to an inflating housing bubble. The Irish banks funneled huge amounts of capital into the housing industry, swelling up their balance sheets. Banks had traditionally relied on domestic deposits to fund loans and mortgages, but with the introduction of the euro currency and a greater risk appetite of foreign investors, the banks were able to attract a huge amount of funds from abroad to feed the housing industry. The loans became more and more risky. The housing market had reached its peak in 2007 (European Commission 2012).

When the bubble burst, the overleveraged banks were facing bankruptcy as mortgage default increased amid falling home prices. The government bailed out the banks, and used public funds to recapitalize the banks and guarantee its liabilities (European Commission 2012). The liability of all Irish banks stood at €575 billion, or 309% of GDP, in February 2009 (White 2009). Anglo-Irish Bank, the largest lender during the property bubble, was nationalized in 2009. The fiscal position of the government deteriorated dramatically with a fall in tax revenues as a result of greater unemployment and foreclosed houses, and bailout programs for banks. Greater unemployment was caused by a sharp contraction in bank lending and falling demand (Lane 2011). The positive budget balance of 2.9% of GDP in 2006 turned into a -30.8% in 2010 during the height of the banking crisis, and had since been reduced to -7.6% in 2012 (cf.

Illustration 18). The very low debt-to-GDP ratio in 2007 of 25% increased to 117.6% in 2012 (cf. Illustration 19).

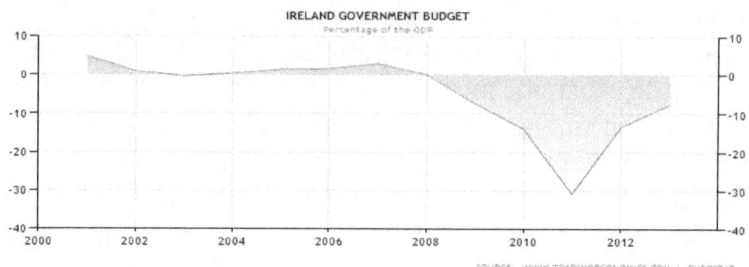

Illustration 18: Ireland Government Budget Balance

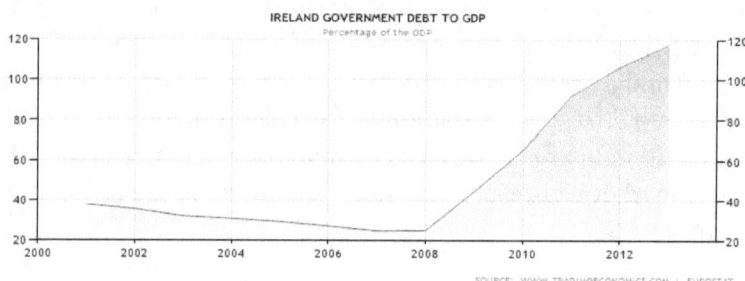

Illustration 19: Ireland Government Debt-to-GDP Ratio

10-year government bond yield increased from a pre-crisis average of about 4% to 14.96% in mid-2011, and has since come down to 4% again as of July 2013.[20] Interest payment on the national debt as percentage of total government revenues increased from 4.1% in 2008 to 10.1% in 2011.[21] In order to counter the debt burden, the Irish government embarked on a €14.6 billion austerity program between 2008 and 2010, which is equivalent to 9.3% of the country's 2010 GDP. In November 2010

---

20 Trading Economics, "Ireland Government Bond 10Y."
   http://www.tradingeconomics.com/ireland/government-bond-yield
21 World Bank, "Interest Payments (% of Revenue)".
   http://data.worldbank.org/indicator/GC.XPN.INTP.RV.ZS

another four year fiscal plan, which would include another €15 billion in austerity, was passed (Lane 2011). Irish annual government spending had peaked at the beginning of 2008 at €7.348 billion, and has been reduced to €5.949 billion in November 2012.[22] But these austerity measures were not enough to handle the debt overhang created by the failed banks. The EU and IMF granted Ireland an €85 billion bailout package in November 2010 in exchange for continued austerity and 5.8% interest per year for a 7.5 year loan (Lane 2011). The budget deficit should be reduced to 3% of GDP in 2015, and the large banks are to be merged. The government has also been instructed to implement "structural reforms", i.e. reducing labor costs and raising competitiveness with a labor market reform (European Commission 2012). As of July 2012, Ireland has returned to the bond market after a lockout of two years (Chaturvedi, Bartha and Quinn 2012).

The austerity measures had started as early as September 2008, when the government under Brian Cowen froze the pay of public-sector workers (Evans-Pritchard 2008). In the same month, the government had guaranteed €440 billion to 6 Irish banks (O'Connor 2011). In February 2009, the government announced a pension levy between 3% for incomes above €15,000 up to 9.6% for incomes above €300,000. Early child care support is cut from €1,100 to €1,000, saving €75 million. €140 million are cut from the general administration. (RTE News 2009). In April 2009, it passed a €3.2 billion austerity program, which includes tax increases and spending cuts (Telegraph 2009). €4 billion were transferred from the national pension fund to secure the bailouts, and another €3 billion for 2010 and 2011 that were dedicated to the pension fund would also go to recapitalize the banks (James 2009). In December 2009, the government facing rising deficits among a declining economy pushed for even steeper budget cuts. Public servants receive 5-8% in pay cuts on salaries below

---

22 Trading Economics, "Ireland Government Spending." http://www.tradingeconomics.com/ireland/government-spending

€125,000, and 15% pay cut for high-salary earners. The government also announced a new property tax (Economist 2009). In the mean time, €30 billion were transferred into the banks (Alderman 2010).

The government had negotiated with the public-sector unions the so-called Croke Park Agreement, in June 2010, which guaranteed no pay cuts and layoffs for public-sector workers in exchange for abstentions from strikes, and reforms to reduce cost and increase flexibility in the workforce. It has so far reduced spending by €1.8 billion since implementation. The public expenditure minister, Brendan Howlin, had announced another €1 billion in additional savings following the civil service reform (O'Connell 2013). The number of public-sector workers was reduced by 28,000 between 2008 and 2012 (Implementation Body 2012), and currently stands at 290,500 (O'Connell 2013). The work week for those working less than 35 hours was increased to 37 hours, and for those working more than 35 hours to 39 or 40 hours. Evening overtime pay was canceled, and Sunday extra pay was cut by 12.5% (Shilton 2013).

The Cowen government unveiled a new austerity plan in November 2010 to qualify for the EU-IMF bailouts. While the 12.5% corporate tax was maintained, value-added taxes were increased from 21% to 22%, and €2 billion were raised by reducing tax breaks for pensioners and levying income taxes on low-income earners. A property tax was levied, and the minimum wage was lowered from €8.65 to €7.65. Besides the cuts in the public wage bill, €3 billion were cut from social spending. Another €3 billion was cut from government investment projects (Shah 2010). As of July 2011, €30 billion worth of austerity measures had been delivered, which is equivalent to a fifth of the nation's GDP (O'Connor 2011). Between 2008 and 2011, capital investments have fallen by 60% (Burke 2012). For the year 2012, the new government under Enda Kenny announced another €3.8 billion in fiscal adjustments, involving tax increases and spending cuts in November 2011 (Department of Finance 2011). The value-added tax was raised to 23%, and welfare payments were further reduced, even as 15% of people were unemployed and 100,000 homeowners had negative equity (Elliott 2011).

In June 2012, a majority of Irish voters voted in favor of the new EU fiscal treaty in a referendum, which subjects Ireland to tough fiscal guidelines coupled with more austerity in exchange for more bailouts and financial assistance from the EU if needed (McKittrick 2012; RTE News 2012). In December 2012, the government announced the sixth austerity budget, involving €2.5 billion in cuts. The overall package was €3.5 billion (Sky News 2012). Property taxes were raised. Home values up to €1 million were taxed at 0.18%, while home values above €1 million were taxed at 0.25%. Child and household benefits were reduced by €10 a month. University tuition fees were to rise by €250 per student, and the motor tax also increased. Wine and cigarette taxes also went up (McDonald 2012). In April 2013, the government announced that austerity involving tax increases and spending cuts will remain in place at least until 2016 (O'Brien 2013).

The austerity policies in Ireland have deteriorated the economy, and weakened consumption, while raising the rate of unemployment. GDP growth turned from -0.4% in 2008, -7.1% in 2009, -2.9% in 2010, -0.1% in 2011, 1.8% in 2012 to -0.9% in March 2013 (cf. Illustration 20). The government had predicted a 2.5% growth rate in 2012, but it turned out to be only 1% (Collins 2013). Ireland has now experienced three quarters of recession in a row (McDonald 2013). The unemployment rate changed from 6% in 2008, 12.3% in 2009, 13.7% in 2010, 14.5% in 2011, 14.9% in 2012 to 13.2% in 2013 (cf. Illustration 21). There has been a small decline in the unemployment rate, but that was because most of the jobs that were created come from part-time jobs. Full-time employment fell by 3,700 between March 2011 and 2012, while part-time employment had increased by 24,200

(O'Brien and Kenny 2013). Domestic demand had been 25.6% below the 2007 peak (Burke 2012). Year-on-year average industrial wages have declined by 3.3% in 2012 (Reilly 2012), which certainly depresses domestic consumption. On the other hand, lower wages have allowed the Irish economy to become more export competitive, leading to more exports into the UK and the US (Doyle 2012). The negative current account balance of -5.7% of GDP in 2008 turned into a positive 2.1% in December 2012.[23]

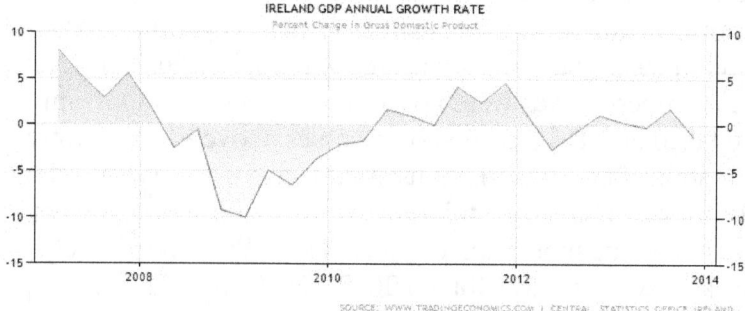
Illustration 20: Ireland Annual GDP Growth Rate

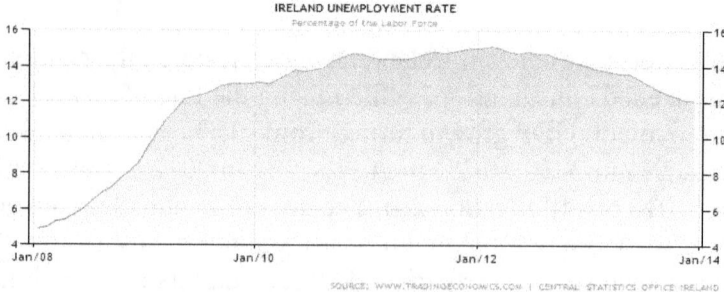
Illustration 21: Ireland Unemployment Rate

Aside from the economic consequences of austerity, the social consequences have been equally dramatic. Cuts in health care funding have reduced medical staff from 111,000 in 2008 to

---

23 Trading Economics, "Ireland Current Account to GDP." http://www.tradingeconomics.com/ireland/current-account-to-gdp

101,000 in mid-2012 (O'Grady 2012, 15). The number of people waiting for hospital treatments has increased by 24% between 2011 and 2012 (Susan Mitchell 2012). Cash-strapped hospitals are sending their patients home during the weekends (NBC News 2012). The recent €90 million cuts in education spending have increased the student-teacher ratio from 1:17 to 1:19, while reducing teaching staff by several hundred (O'Regan 2013). The homeless rate dramatically increased in Ireland, even though 289,451 properties are vacant following the property boom (Ryan 2012). Homeless charity had a 62% increase in homeless residents between 2009 and 2011.

Ireland reduced health care coverage for people over 70. Prescription drug costs for low-income groups have increased, and twice as many people go without health care because they can't afford it. Suicide rates increased 24% between 2007 and 2009, and rose again by 27% in 2010 (Fitzpatrick 2013). Austerity and a bad labor market have induced many young Irish people to emigrate. Over 300,000 people have left since the onset of the crisis, and another 75,000 are expected to leave in 2013, out of a total working population of 2.16 million (Petras 2013). While most crimes have decreased during the downturn, burglaries have increased by 17%[24] and prostitution has increased by 36% since 2007.[25] Unlike the Spanish or the Greeks, the Irish have been relatively restrained when it comes to social protests, though, there had been several anti-austerity protests (e.g. Haughey 2010; Mangan 2013)

With austerity so clearly failing in Ireland, the argument had

---

24 Central Statistics Office, "Burglary and Related Offences." http://www.cso.ie/Quicktables/GetQuickTables.aspx?FileName=cja01c12.asp&TableName=Burglary+and+related+offences&StatisticalProduct=DB_CJ

25 Central Statistics Office, "Public Order and Other Social Code Offences." http://www.cso.ie/Quicktables/GetQuickTables.aspx?FileName=cja01c18.asp&TableName=Public+order+and+other+social+code+offences&StatisticalProduct=DB_CJ

been advanced that Irish fiscal consolidation in the 1980s had led to economic growth (Giavazzi and Pagano 1990). The implication of this type of reasoning is that what had served Ireland so well back in the 1980s, might also work to overcome the current crisis. However, Ireland's economy had recovered in the 1980s during a period of growth in the international economy, subsidies from the EU upon membership accession, wage increases for public-sector workers, and currency devaluation (Kinsella 2011). Ireland's ensuing export boom was also benefited by the fact that it had a relatively small economy (Jayadev and Konczal 2010). None of these things are available for the current economic crisis. Ireland as part of the eurozone may not have experienced any currency shocks, but it is also unable to devalue its currency and relieve economic pressure. With the logic of internal devaluation, the austerity policies involving pay cuts, reductions in social services and a decrease in capital investment projects, have exacerbated the economic crisis.

Chapter 7: United Kingdom

Britain is different from the other six eurozone countries that I have discussed so far. It is not part of the eurozone, and can cope with economic distress and increased debt burden by devaluing its currency rather than by internal deflation, i.e. by austerity policies to reduce domestic living standards. The UK, unlike many other peripheral eurozone countries, had significant leeway to resolve its debt crisis. It also has the privilege of not having the IMF or the EU interfere in its economic policy-making. Britain's borrowing costs have also been reduced following the turmoil in the eurozone. 10-year government bonds averaged 5% between the late-1990s and the crisis in 2008, but had since been reduced to 2.62% in July 2013.[26] It is, therefore, noteworthy that the UK has nonetheless chosen the latter solution. Britain had "led the way in voluntary deficit reduction" and "it is now enduring a prolonged period of near-stagnation", thus carrying out more years of austerity than planned (Giles and Bounds 2012). But how did Britain get on the path of austerity? There is a political answer to this question. Austerity began with the premiership of David Cameron (Conservative Party) in May 2010.

When Gordon Brown (Labour Party) took over his premiership in June 2007, there were no indications that reducing the fiscal deficit would be the exclusive concern of the UK government. At that time, the UK economy began to flounder, and the overleveraged banks sitting on enormous debts they had incurred from risky investments[27] requested bailouts from the government. In October 2008, the government passed a £500 billion bank rescue package, the biggest in history (Winnett and Porter 2008).

---

26 Trading Economics, "United Kingdom Government Bond 10Y." http://www.tradingeconomics.com/united-kingdom/government-bond-yield
27 For a discussion of the cause of the banking crisis in the UK, consider House of Commons (2009). The Bank of England chairman, Mervyn King, argues that low-interest rate policies, and economic imbalances between US/UK and China/Asia had encouraged more speculation and more debt bubbles (ibid., 12-13).

As the economy was deteriorating, the debts were piling up as the unemployment rate and unemployment compensation increased and tax revenues fell, and bank bailouts burdened the treasury. But rather than embark on austerity, the Brown government pushed for fiscal stimulus. In November 2008, the government announced £20 billion worth of tax cuts (though tax rates were increased for high-income earners), and the value-added tax was reduced from 17.5% to 15%; child benefits were set to increase; pensioners got a £60 one-off payment; £150 million in energy saving measures such as home insulation were invested (Totaro 2008). In January 2009, the government gave £20 billion in loan guarantees to small and medium businesses to help them survive the economic downturn (BBC 2009a).

In April 2009, the government announced a budget that raised alcohol, tobacco and fuel taxes, but at the same time provided £2,000 in tax benefits for car purchases. Income taxes for those earning more than £150,000 were set to rise to 50%. Statutory redundancy pay was increased from £350 to £380 per week; under-25 year olds who had been out of work for a year were offered a job or training place; job centers received £1.7 billion more in funding; £500 million were dedicated for stalled housing projects; £1 billion were dedicated to fund low-carbon industries; tax refunds for businesses making losses were expanded; state pensions were increased by 2.5% (BBC 2009b). In April 2009, the amount of paid vacation was increased from 4.8 weeks to 5.6 weeks a year; an anti-discrimination law came into effect. In October 2009, the minimum wage rate was raised from £5.73 to £5.80 (Prosser 2011).

In December 2009, chancellor of the exchequer (finance minister), Alistair Darling, announced that the recession was worse than anticipated, with GDP shrinking by 4.75% rather than the earlier estimate of 3.5%; and fiscal deficits were £178 billion rather than £175 billion as predicted. Darling further announced a two-year cap on public-sector wage rises of 1%; bank bonuses over £25,000 would be taxed; the pension insurance contributions were raised. But the government did not go full-scale into austerity. A job-training program was guaranteed to people below age 24; corporation tax increases were deferred for one year; state pensions were set to rise by 2.5%; free school meals to low-income children were expanded; and tax rebates for electric cars and wind turbines were expanded (BBC 2009c).

For the election campaign in April 2010, the Brown government announced a continuous increase in the minimum wage; free nursery places; education guarantees to children up to age 18; a toddler tax credit of £4 extra per week; an increase in paternity leave to four weeks; and no stamp-duty for fist-time home buyers for houses below £250,000 value for the first two years. During the Brown government (2007-10), the budget deficit increased from -2.7% in 2007, -5.1% in 2008, -11.2% in 2009 to -10.2% in 2010 (cf. Illustration 22)[28], while the debt-to-GDP ratio was raised from 44.5% in 2007 to 80% in 2010 (cf. Illustration 23).[29]

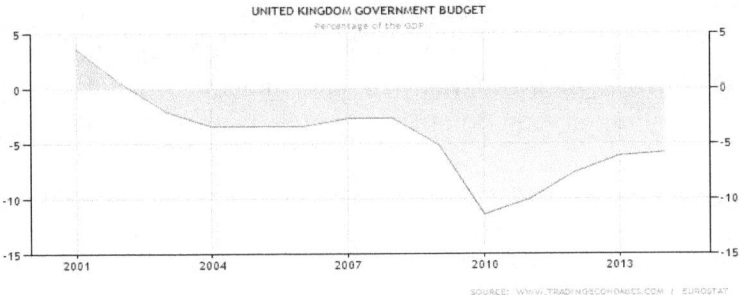

Illustration 22: United Kingdom Government Budget Balance

---

28 Trading Economics, "United Kingdom Government Budget."
http://www.tradingeconomics.com/united-kingdom/government-budget
29 Trading Economics, "United Kingdom Government Debt to GDP."
http://www.tradingeconomics.com/united-kingdom/government-debt-to-gdp

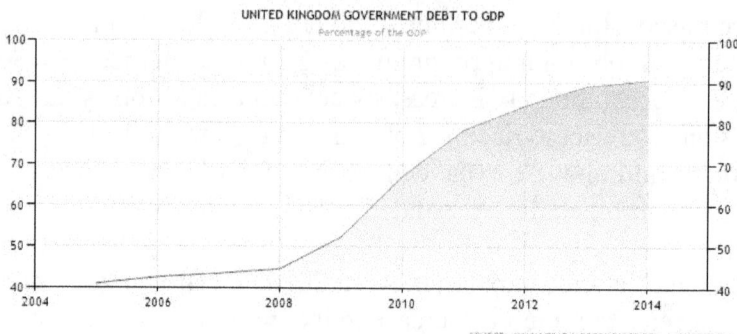

Illustration 23: United Kingdom Government Debt-to-GDP Ratio

But with a continuing negative fiscal outlook and poor economic performance, prime minister Brown's Labour Party lost his re-election bid. In May 2010, David Cameron from the Conservative Party negotiated a coalition government with the Liberal Democrats. The new prime minister, Cameron, and his chancellor of the exchequer, George Osborne, were elected on a platform of austerity. The Tories argued that with high fiscal deficits, the UK became less and less capable of repaying the debts. Before going bankrupt, the government has to dramatically curb spending in order to bring deficit and debt under control.

Cameron's government held true the implicit assumption that changes in government spending policies have no effect on economic activity and unemployment, which is a perspective that Keynes called the "Treasury view" (Wolf 2010). If the government can not affect economic activity and if, in addition, government taxing and spending programs have the tendency to crowd out private spending, then it is the duty of the government not to stimulate the economy, but to pull back on spending to revive market confidence. Following the assumption that government spending cuts are offset by private-sector spending, the government had cut out many public-sector workers in the anticipation that the private-sector would increase hiring. But between June 2010, when the conservative government took office, and March 2012, 44,000 more public-sector jobs have been lost than created in the private-sector (Blanchflower 2012).

Chancellor George Osborne immediately went to work in May 2010 by announcing a £6.2 billion spending cut program, announcing cutbacks in the number of government offices, less spending on consultancy and IT projects, a civil service recruitment freeze, a cut in the child trust fund (saving account for children, where the government invests £250 per child after child birth and at age 7). The lower-level administrations in Scotland, Wales and Northern Ireland faced £704 million in cuts, while local authorities were receiving £1.17 billion in cuts; £320 million were axed from the youth employment program; extra university places were cut from 20,000 to 10,000. Osborne justified these sweeping cuts by arguing that "we need to take urgent action to keep our interest rates lower for longer, to boost confidence in the economy, and protect jobs to show the world we can live within our means. We need to tackle the deficit so that our debt repayments don't spiral out of control. And the more we do now the more we can spend on the things that really matter in the years ahead." (BBC 2010a). These combined austerity measures were expected to cut out 1.3 million jobs (Elliott 2010).

In June 2010, Osborne announced an increase in the value-added tax from 17.5% to 20%; a freezing of child benefits, and public-sector pay above £21,000 a year; a 25% cut of public service spending; housing benefits were limited to a maximum of £400 a week (saving £1.9 billion); tax allowances were raised and low-income taxpayers receive a £200 tax cut (BBC 2010c). By July 2010, 80 non-government agencies receiving public funding had been axed. With regard to the employees that were slated to lose their jobs, ministers hoped "that a recovering private sector will offer them jobs" (Morris 2010), even though British corporations were holding £754 billion in cash rather than creating jobs (Warner 2012). A total of 192 such public bodies were axed, and 118 were merged (BBC 2010d). In October 2010, the chancellor presented a spending review until 2014-15, which included the programs to be cut in this austerity drive: 490,000 public-sector jobs were made redundant; departments would receive 19% cuts in four years; £7 billion were removed from the welfare budget; the police budget was cut by 4% per year; the retirement age was increased from 65 to 66 until 2020; school budgets were protected; social care received a boost of £2 billion; the national health service budget was permitted to increase until 2015; rail fares would be hiked; bank levies were made permanent (BBC 2010e). In June 2011, the IMF praised Britain's path of fiscal consolidation, even though economic growth rates were scaled back from a predicted 1.7% in March 2011 to 1.5% (Hannon 2011). Faced with a quarterly growth of 0.2% in 2011, chancellor Osborne justified the austerity policies to reduce the debt, arguing that "abandoning [fiscal austerity] now would only risk British jobs and growth" (Aldrick 2011). In August 2011, the National Institute for Economic and Social Research countered Britain's austerity policies will make the fiscal crisis worse, because weak growth rates following austerity will make the government fail to reach the fiscal targets (Keiller and Elliott 2011).

With the economic outlook deteriorating, the government in November 2011 announced to extend the austerity policies from 2015 to 2017, and borrow £111 billion between 2011 and 2015. The public-sector payroll was slashed by 600,000 employees; public-sector worker pay was capped with 1% increases (Werdigier 2011). In March 2012, Osborne announced the annual budget, which includes a freeze on tax-free allowances for people over 65, saving £3.5 billion from the treasury, and leaving 5 million pensioners worse off. 700,000 people who turned 65 were losing £323 annually (Hall 2012). The average pensioner lost £84 per year. £10 billion were cut from the welfare budget. At the same time, the government reduced the top income tax rate from 50% to 45%, benefiting the richest 300,000 households in Britain while lowering government revenues by £100 million. On the other side, income tax allowances for low-income earners increased and raises treasury costs by £3 billion. Tax cuts for corporations cost £730 million, which the government expected to increase investments and encourage business hiring (even as companies are reluctant to hire due to a weak economy) (Wintour and Elliott 2012).

By the end of 2012, it became clear that the UK had slid into a double-dip recession with nine consecutive months of negative growth (Bryan-Low 2012). A new budget with somewhat less austerity was announced in March 2013 with a deficit forecast of 7.4% of GDP, which is greater than the 6.9% forecast three months prior, while public sector debt was 75.9% as opposed to 74.7% in the previous forecast. GDP growth was 0.6%, even though the previous forecast predicted 1.2% in growth. With regard to the policies being implemented, the personal allowance are to be raised to £10,000 (tax exemption for low-income workers); corporate taxes were reduced from 21% to 20% in April 2015; bank levy was increased to 0.142%; a crackdown on tax evasion was designed to raise £3 billion; tax-free child care vouchers of £1,200 per child was introduced; a flat-rate for pensions of £144 per week was introduced; the savings on government departments were raised from £10 billion to £11.5 (excluding health, education and foreign aid); public-sector pay cap of 1% was extended to 2016; the cap on social care costs was reduced from £75,000 to £72,000, but the threshold for means-tested care was raised from £23,000 to £118,000 (Owen 2013).

Chancellor Osborne in March 2013 announced an extension of austerity cuts until 2018 (Vina, Hutton and Penny 2013). The average family is £891 worse off due to cuts effective April 1, 2013. Due to tighter eligibility requirements for benefits, 3.7 million disabled people will lose £28 billion by 2018 in benefit cuts (Moss and Glaze 2013). In June 2013, the government announced more austerity to be implemented in 2015, which included cuts in local government funding and the justice budget by 10%. On the other hand, spending on capital projects for roads and railways will rise by £50 billion (Thomson 2013). In addition, welfare payments were reduced, while public-sector pay increases are curbed. Unemployed persons will be obliged to visit a job center every week rather than every second week, and unemployment benefits do not kick in immediately upon unemployment, but after seven days of active job search (Castle 2013).

The UK's austerity policies since 2010 predictably had a small impact toward reducing deficits, while continuing to increase the total debt burden and dragging down economic growth. The elevated unemployment rate has not been brought down since the conservative government had been in office. The Brown government's -10.2% budget deficit of GDP was reduced to a -6.3% deficit in December 2012.[30] Government debt-to-GDP ratio increased from 80% in 2010 to 90.7% in 2012.[31] The annual GDP growth rate changed from 2.7% in 2008, -6.1% in 2009, 1.2% in 2010, 1.4% in 2011, 0.5% in 2012 to 0.3% in March 2013 (cf. Illustration 24). The unemployment rate changed from 5.4% in 2008, 7.4% in 2009, 8.1% in 2010, 7.8% in 2011, 8.2% in 2012 to 7.8% in April 2013 (cf. Illustration 25). Britain's export economy has not been helped by the austerity policies or by currency devaluation of 20% (Warner 2013). The current account balance had been continuously negative at least since 1984, and was -3.7% of GDP as of 2012.[32] British workers had, nonetheless, lost 6% of income since 2008. Between 2010 to 2011, 70% of employees, who stayed in the same job experienced real wage

---

30 Trading Economics, "United Kingdom Government Budget."
http://www.tradingeconomics.com/united-kingdom/government-budget
31 Trading Economics, "United Kingdom Government Debt to GDP."
http://www.tradingeconomics.com/united-kingdom/government-debt-to-gdp
32 Trading Economics, "United Kingdom Current Account to GDP." Trading Economics, "United Kingdom Government Debt to GDP."
http://www.tradingeconomics.com/united-kingdom/current-account-to-gdp

cuts. Labor union membership declined from 37% of the workforce in the early-1980s to 19% in 2008 (RT 2013).

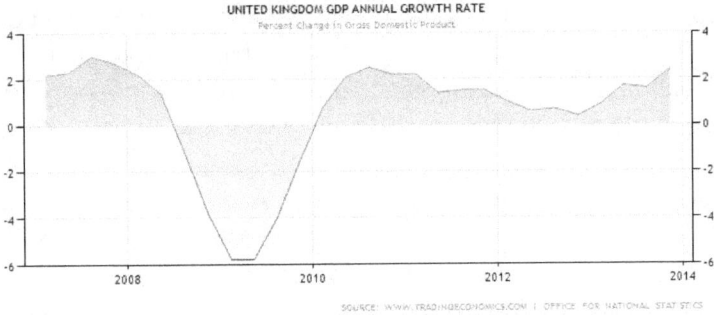
Illustration 24: United Kingdom Annual GDP Growth Rate

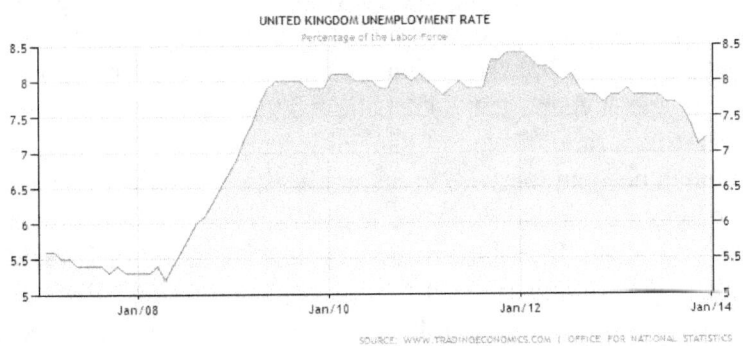
Illustration 25: United Kingdom Unemployment Rate

The human consequences of austerity had been significant: One report says that 33% of British households lacked at least three basic living necessities, such as heated homes, healthy food, basic clothing items, in 2012, compared with 14% in 1983 (Butler and Gentleman 2013). 4.82 million workers are paid less than a living wage of £8.30 an hour in London and £7.20 in the rest of the country (RT 2012). In 2012, there had been a 42% increase in homelessness, forcing some people to sleep in caves, as homeless shelters are unable to keep them in shelters (Telegraph 2013). Using empty properties as means of shelter has been complicated by the introduction of an anti-squatter law, that prohibits squatters under threat of up to six months jail-time and fines of up to £5,000, and has put several people to jail even as 930,000 properties across the UK were empty and not in use (Bowcott 2012). The demand for emergency food banks tripled between 2012 and 2013, especially since the welfare cuts in April 2013 were implemented (Morris 2013).

The introduction of a bedroom tax in April 2013, which includes cuts in welfare benefits for every extra spare room that poor people own, had caused economic hardship for the affected families by putting these families into payment arrears (Harris 2013). A survey that asked 300 UK doctors in 2012 reveals the extent of the social costs of austerity: 76% of GP's (general practitioners) believe that the economic downturn had negative effects on their patients. 64% believe that their patients consumed more alcohol; 60% believe that patients were canceling sporting activities to save money; 34% believed that patients were putting off starting a family due to financial insecurity; 77% believe that there had been an increase in mental health conditions linked to the economic climate (Kunzmann 2012). The health care system cuts have also affected the quality of health care that UK residents could get. The National Health Service, which is considered to be among the best ranked health care systems in the world based on the public provision of services (Adams 2011), is slated to cut £20 billion from the budget between 2011 and 2015, leading to restrictions in care eligibility, extended wait times for surgeries and treatments and 20,000 health staff cuts (Cheng 2011). Enormous cuts in the higher education budget have forced universities to triple their tuition fees to £9,000 a year (Marcus 2011). All these austerity measures have produced some public reaction in the form of protests and demonstrations (e.g. CNN 2012; Morrison 2012; Kilkenny 2013).

Chapter 8: Latvia

Latvia is an odd case. It has carried out harsh austerity measures following the financial and economic crisis in 2008, and has rebounded with high growth rates. Among some people, Latvia has been used as an example for other countries to follow. It is used as an example for how austerity works to return a country to economic prosperity while lowering debt thanks to greater investor confidence (e.g. Aslund and Dombrovskis 2011; Aslund 2012; Tanner 2012 ; Bandow 2013). Matthew Yglesias, for example, lauded Latvia's effort to carry out austerity policies that were dictated by EU officials to secure Latvia's accession to the eurozone, and called it a success story. "[The Latvian success story is] a reminder of what's genuinely fantastic about the European Union and its amazing success at creating a framework in which Europe's nations can live in peace, Europe's smaller nations can enjoy an unprecedented level of security, and where the lure of EU expansion has helped consolidate liberal democratic institutions in large swathes of eastern and central Europe" (Yglesias 2013). The Latvian prime minister, Valdis Dombrovskis, who saw his country recovering in September 2011, said that "I think it's really in Greece's interest to actually go ahead with this [austerity] package ... The point is that financial stability is the pre-condition for economic growth" (Adomaitis and Shanley 2011). Can Latvia be taken as a good example and role model for the other struggling eurozone countries to be copied?

I will first outline how Latvia's economic crisis came about, and what the austerity policies were. Then I will assess the economic data for the impact of austerity policies on the Latvian economy, and conclude that these policies had been a failure. After the fall of the Soviet Union and Latvia's independence, Soviet-era plants shut down, destroying the industrial base of the country (Higgins 2013). A few Latvian businessmen became very rich as a result of facilitating currency exchanges and accepting deposits with very few regulations. In 1995, the Banka Baltija went under. It had bet on the devaluation of the Latvian currency, the lats, and promised depositors a 90% return. When the bank collapsed, depositors lost all of their deposits, and the country plunged into an economic crisis. In 1998, a financial crisis in Russia rocked the deposits of the Riga Commerce Bank, and a bailout through the European Bank for Reconstruction and Development (ERBD) rescued it. It was in this year that foreign capital, especially from the Scandinavian countries entered the country. Examples are SEB (Sweden), Swedbank (Sweden), DnB ORD (Norway), Nordea (Finland) and Norvik (Iceland) (OCCRP 2011).

Since then Latvia's economy and those of other Eastern European countries were built on strong foreign capital inflows, mainly from Western European banks, who transferred enormous assets into Latvia and other Eastern European states, which went to feed an expansion of consumption and a housing boom. When the boom turned to bust, as borrowers defaulted on their loan, enormous capital flight weakened Latvia's economy. In 2008, the largest bank, Parex Bank, was taken over by the government. Latvia's economy shrunk by 20% in 2009, government and private-sector debt expanded, banking crisis, and falling competitiveness were harming the economy and society (Higgins 2013). A -0.4% national deficit of GDP in 2007 turned into a -9.8% deficit in 2009, but had since been reduced to -1.2% in 2012 (cf. Illustration 26).[33] The debt-to-GDP ratio increased from 9% in 2007 to 44.4% in 2010, but has been reduced to 40.7% in 2012 (cf. Illustration 27).[34] As a result of greater government debt, the share of government revenues going to debt service increased from 1.3% in 2008 to 4.5% in 2011.[35] In order to handle the bank bailouts, Latvia received a €7.5 billion bailout in December 2008

---

33 Trading Economics, "Latvia Government Budget."
http://www.tradingeconomics.com/latvia/government-budget
34 Trading Economics, "Latvia Government Debt to GDP."
http://www.tradingeconomics.com/latvia/government-debt-to-gdp
35 World Bank, "Interest Payments (% of Revenue)."
http://data.worldbank.org/indicator/GC.XPN.INTP.RV.ZS

from the EU (Eglitis 2008). A January 2009 agreement in Vienna guaranteed that Western European bank assets would remain in Latvia if the country would continue to peg the Latvian currency to the euro and commit to internal deflation, i.e. austerity, to prevent the banking system from absorbing any losses (EBRD 2012; Blyth 2013a, 219-221).

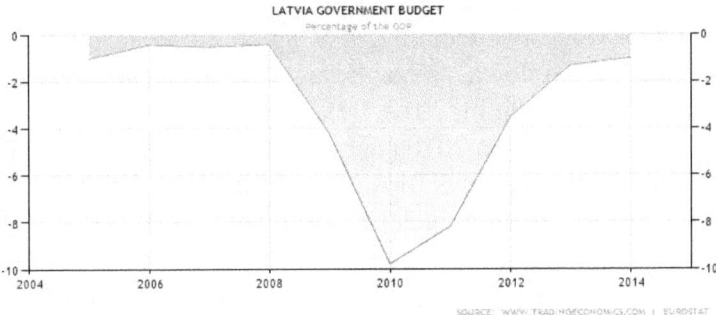

Illustration 26: Latvia Government Budget Balance

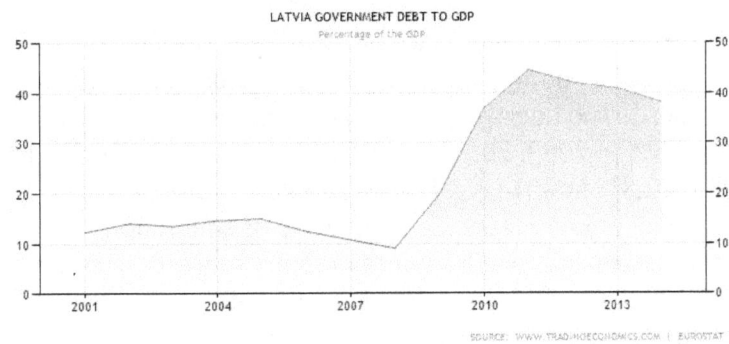

Illustration 27: Latvia Government Debt-to-GDP Ratio

The Latvian government under the leadership of Valdis Dombrovskis, implemented austerity measures rather than currency devaluation to boost exports, because it wanted to gain credibility among EU officials that it wanted to become part of the eurozone.[36] It also wanted to avoid any losses to the banks during the financial crisis. The major banks held enormous sway in EU policy-making, and ensured that any provisions demanded by the EU from the Latvian government would not threaten the banks' assets (Weisbrot and Ray 2011, 8). Spending cuts and tax increases were all implemented in 2009, and consisted of 15% of GDP. The number of public employees was reduced by 30%, public-sector wages were cut by 22%, 35 out of 59 hospitals and 100 schools closed down. Average wages fell by 13.6% between 2008 and 2010 (Lindholm 2012, 99). Austerity measures were limited to 4% of GDP in 2010 (Economist 2010). In 2010, income taxes increased and ceilings for social and unemployment benefits were created. State family benefits, child birth benefits were reduced; eligibility to parental benefits was restricted to non-working parents; income assessment to qualify for the minimum income was made stricter and its benefit amount was reduced. For 2011, the austerity measures were 2.6% of GDP. Social security contributions were increased (Rastrigina and Zasova 2012).

The question is whether all these austerity measures have improved the economy. On the face of it, the unemployment rate was reduced. The unemployment rate changed from 6.8% in 2008, 14.3% in 2009, 20.7% in 2010, 17.6% in 2011, 16.3% in 2012, to 12.8% in 2013 (cf. Illustration 28). But the declining unemployment rate masks the huge wave of emigration that afflicted Latvia. The harsh austerity regime succeeded largely without much public protest, because 10% of Latvians had emigrated since 2004. The exodus accelerated after the economy collapsed in 2008. Latvia's population declined from 2.7 million in 1991 to 2.08 million in 2010 (Sommers and Hudson 2013). A look at the GDP figures also give the deceptive impression that austerity was beneficial to the economy. GDP growth changed from 9% in 2007, 0.8% in 2008, -17.8% in 2009, -6.1% in 2010, 3.5% in 2011, 6.9% in 2012 to 3.6% in 2013 (cf. Illustration 29).

---

36 This bid had been successful, because Latvia will introduce the euro in 2014 (Paterson 2013).

The positive growth figures give the impression that the austerity medicine of 2009 had worked. However, a comparison between Latvia's economy, and those of Iceland, the UK and the US, shows that Latvia, while recording huge growth rates since 2011, is not even close to reaching the pre-recession level GDP (cf. Illustration 30).

Furthermore, the export-led recovery is weakening due to continuing stagnation in Europe (Lindholm 2012, 99) Consumption as share of the total economy had been decreasing, contributing to a lower growth in GDP than what could otherwise be expected if the austerity policies had not brought down wages and consumption. In 2008, household consumption decreased by -4.8%, in 2009 by -23.7%, and in 2010 increased by 0.6%.[37] In addition, currency devaluation would have had milder consequences on economic contraction than austerity. The average loss for countries that carried out devaluation during a crisis was 4.5% of GDP. Latvia, however, lost 24.1% of GDP during the recession . Latvia enormously weakened austerity measures in 2010, and had experienced a slow recovery ever since. Rising inflation reduced borrowing costs and debts, allowing the government to raise fiscal spending. The export sector only marginally contributed to economic growth due to correspondingly rising imports (Weisbrot and Ray 2011). The 2008 current account deficit of -22.3% of GDP, however, was reduced to -2.5% in 2012.[38]

---

37 World Bank, "Household Final Consumption Expenditure per Capita Growth (annual %)."
http://data.worldbank.org/indicator/NE.CON.PRVT.PC.KD.ZG
38 Trading Economics, "Latvia Current Account to GDP."
http://www.tradingeconomics.com/latvia/current-account-to-gdp

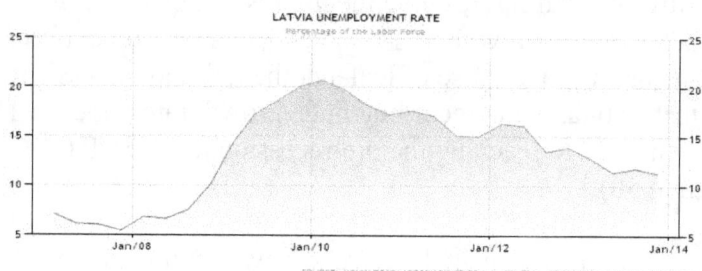
Illustration 28: Latvia Unemployment Rate

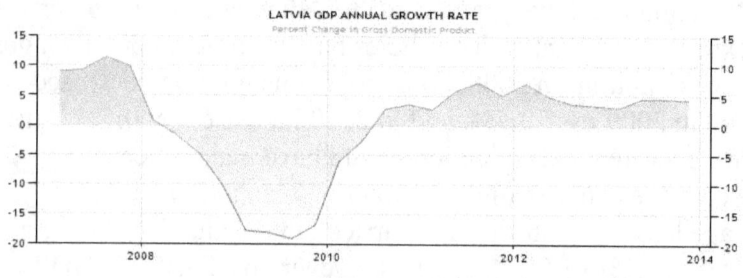
Illustration 29: Latvia Annual GDP Growth

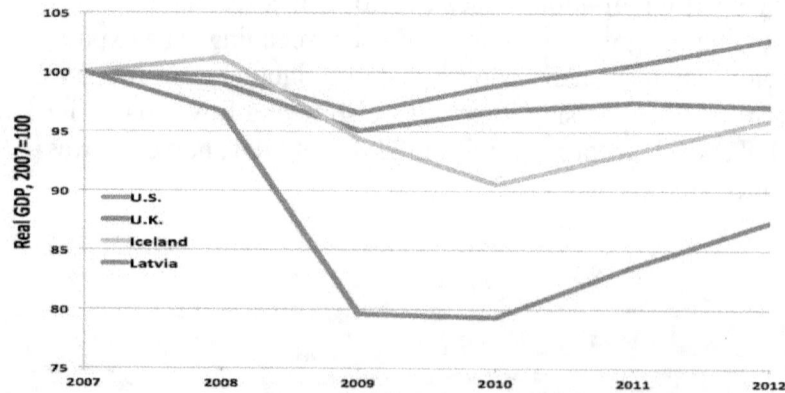
Illustration 30: Latvia's Real GDP in Comparison with the U.S., U.K. and Iceland

Latvia was not a success story, because the social costs had been enormous: the poverty rate increased from 33.8% in 2008 to

36.6% in 2012.[39] Latvia also remains the second most unequal society in Europe (though inequality decreased slightly since 2008) (Babones 2012). The higher education budget was cut by 48% in 2009 and another 18% in 2010 (Zitko 2012), indicating a greater burden on students to carry the costs of higher education. Latvia also cut its health care budget by 30% between 2008 and 2010 (Fleming 2012). These cuts have led to increases in user charges and reductions in health coverage (Karanikolos et al. 2013). Treatment in clinics have been curtailed. Transportation cuts of 21% involve the elimination of 235 intercity routes and 570 rural routes; some bus terminals were also on the chopping block (Karnite 2011).

Suicide rates are among the highest in Europe; preventable deaths and disabilities increased; road deaths due to drunk driving increased; the crime rate following a greater unemployment rate and police budget cuts increased; and brain drain (emigration of talented people) following education budget cuts and unemployment is weakening the economy (Hudson and Sommers 2012). Though Latvians have been remarkably quiet as a result of the austerity measures, some coordinated protests among students, police officers, transport workers, and farmers, among others, took place (Karnite 2011). Austerity produced more economic and social pain in Latvia than necessary, and can, therefore, not be called a success story.

---

39 Eurostat, "People at Risk of Poverty or Social Exclusion." http://epp.eurostat.ec.europa.eu/portal/page/portal/income_social_inclusion _living_conditions/data/database

Chapter 9: The Argument on Austerity

After the examination of austerity policies across the European continent, I will theoretically debunk the idea that austerity will lead to improvements in the export sector and in the economy via increased investor and consumer confidence. I will also reject the claim that a high debt burden will yield in lower growth rates.

With regard to improving the export sector, the assumption is that if wages are pressed low enough, then exports will be encouraged, because the products that are produced in the country can be sold more cheaply abroad. There are several weaknesses to the argument. First, if the products that a country is producing are not popular in the export market to begin with, then a cheapening of labor costs might not effect an improvement in the export sector. The consistently negative trade balances of Spain and Portugal show that it is enormously difficult for a weak-exporting country to suddenly become major exporters.

Second, the argument neglects the fact that different countries have different rates of productivity. In order to reach the same level of competitiveness, the Greeks would need to have lower real wages than the more productive Germans (lower than even now), which raises the question of social fairness.

Third, the assumption is that the global economy is in an expansionary state. If the economy is contracting, and financial markets are unwilling to undertake significant investments in the real economy, then cheaper products are purchased by no other party.

Fourth, if all countries cut their wage bill at the same time, then it is a race to the bottom (ILO 2012b; Onaran and Galanis 2012). Temporary export improvements of one country are immediately canceled by a global slowdown in demand. Greece is a case in point, because its sharply contracting economy is correlated with a sharp fall in private consumption.

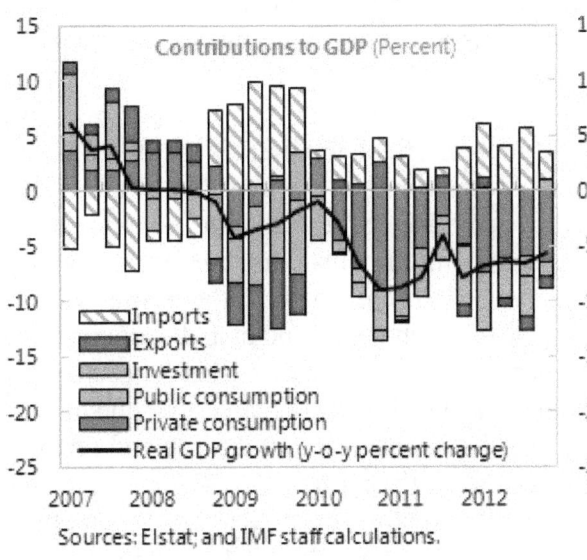

Illustration 31: Greece: Contributions to GDP

Illustration 31 shows the contributions of the various sources of GDP in Greece between 2007 and 2012. The bars shaded in blue shows the annual change in private consumption, and the solid black line shows the change in the real GDP. The real GDP slumped along with a sharp fall in private consumption.

Fifth, not all countries can run current account surpluses at the same time. The export advantages of some countries, such as Saudi Arabia, Germany and China, need to be counter-balanced by the deficit of another country, which traditionally has been the US, UK, India, France, Spain, Italy and Greece. As Guillen and Ontiveros (2012) write, "In the absence of inter-planetary trade, the deficits of some countries need to be compensated by the surpluses of an equivalent magnitude in other countries"(p.10). In the ideal scenario, the states that have run account surpluses can allow deficits every once in a while by using the foreign exchanges to increase the import bill, while other states that are currently running account deficits can raise their export bill to reduce a negative balance. But such smooth development is very unrealistic, because the export champions have no reason to give up their advantageous status, while the net importers find it difficult to raise their exports or minimize their imports. But, in any case, exhorting the peripheral eurozone countries to raise their export profile is unrealistic if some countries have to run deficits.

The other argument of the austerity supporters is that these measures will inspire confidence among the investors, which will improve the economy, because they believe that the government will be able to keep its debt commitments (Graham 1998, 194; Monson and Subramaniam 2010). This logic works insofar as that investor confidence was lost, when the financial and economic crisis broke out in the peripheral eurozone countries (Greece, Portugal, Spain, Italy and Ireland) investors feared that due to the spiking debt load, these governments would not be able to repay them at their value (Menendez 2012). The investors are subsequently inclined to demand a higher interest rate to lend to the more risky countries, arguably exacerbating the payment position of the states further.

But the decisive issue is not how the state debt came into being, and how the investor reaction might be justified.[40] The decisive question I am investigating is whether the austerity measures, which immediately reduces government spending and raises taxes, can contribute to lower debt and an economic recovery. Austerity measures do not reduce debt, but increase it. If all the European countries are simultaneously pulling back on government spending, then the economy will shrink and not grow, because each country is each other's customer. France is the prime destination for German exports, and Germany is the prime destination for Dutch exports. If the income that a country can generate shrinks, then it will have lower tax revenues, and ends up with more debt, even though it saved some money when it

---

40 I do not think that they were justified, because the crisis could have been contained if the investors kept the interest rate low, or if a greater default would have been permitted.

started with the austerity. The people become worse off without the virtue of saving having effected a reduction in debt and an improvement in the economy (Blyth 2013b). With regard to investor confidence, it can only increase if the objective economic environment can justify a greater willingness of investors to purchase government bonds. If the economic environment and the state fiscal position deteriorates, then investors have no interest to lower the interest rate for government bonds, and they will be even less inclined to purchase these bonds at a given interest rate.

If the austerity measures are not likely to increase investor confidence due to a depressed economic situation resulting from austerity, then it is not very likely that they can raise consumer confidence. However, the supporters of the expansionary fiscal contraction hypothesis, Giavazzi and Pagano (1990), claim that government spending cuts, i.e. austerity, will increase consumer confidence, because consumers will spend more money in anticipation of future lower taxes.[41] This claim has been empirically rejected, indicating that fiscal contraction, i.e. government spending cuts, will depress the economy rather than improve it (e.g. Guajardo, Leigh and Pescatori 2011). Research by Alesina and Ardagna (1998, 2010) and Alesina and Perotti (1995, 1997) finds that a policy of government spending cuts rather than tax increases[42] is not contractionary and can instead be

---

41 For a literature review and discussion of expansionary austerity, consider Frankel (2013).

42 The economists have an apparent preference for spending cuts over tax increases with the assumption that high government spending tends to "crowd out" private spending and private investment. It is, furthermore, assumed that tax increases would also diminish the likelihood of private investments. In my view, this perspective has a clear class bias. If the government raises taxes it can decide which class to lay the burden on: a value-added tax hurts middle and lower class people, and capital gains taxes and progressive income taxes hurt upper class people. But with regard to spending cuts, the main targets are middle class civil servants and social programs, which make up a major share of government spending. Spending cuts disproportionately hurt the lower and middle classes much more than tax increases.

expansionary.[43] However, one co-author of the paper, Roberto Perotti, changed his mind in a later paper, and argued that fiscal consolidation only worked in countries that coupled government austerity with currency devaluation and export increases, thus putting into question the expansionary fiscal contraction hypothesis (Perotti 2011).

Eyraud and Weber (2013) argue that fiscal consolidation increases the short-term debt due to a decline of output, i.e. overall GDP. A declining output will usually lead to a fall in investments, an increase in the unemployment rate and a fall in wages, which all contribute to lower consumer confidence. Any expectation of lower taxes in the future are canceled by a depressed economic environment, which forces the states to pursue more austerity in the form of both spending cuts and tax increases. This even puts into question the hypothesis that taxes will, in fact, be lowered in the future.[44] And, besides, it is unlikely that people will spend more money in anticipation of lower taxes if they see the unemployment rate going up as a result of public-sector layoffs, and the social programs cut on which they depend on. It is also questionable whether consumers are so calculating about government policies when it comes to consumer choices.

With regard to fiscal consolidation it should also be noted that cuts in government expenditures, have a negative impact on the

---

43 Alberto Alesina is a very interesting and important economist within the austerity debate. Back in 2010 when the debt crisis was breaking out in full swing, he explained to EU policy makers and finance ministers that "large, credible and decisive spending cuts to reduce budget deficits have frequently been followed by economic growth" (Coy 2010). Europe, indeed, embarked on austerity thereafter with enormously contractionary effects.

44 It seems to be that the proponents of the expansionary fiscal contraction hypothesis assume that the economy remains stable or continues to grow, while the austerity policies are implemented. However, because austerity leads to a contraction in the economy (or an exacerbation of it), thus violating the assumption of the hypothesis, it can not be assumed that taxes will be lower in the future, but higher.

wage share (Loungani 2011), and increases income inequality (Mulas-Granados 2005). Such developments counter the hypothesis that austerity will improve consumer confidence, because a declining wage share is associated with a lower ability of the masses of workers to consume and a lower consumer confidence. It is also important to point out the difference between investor confidence and consumer confidence. Investors often have a choice whether they want to purchase government bonds or corporate stocks or other assets. While in an unfavorable environment, they might refrain from investments, they might still make targeted investments in a country despite its gloomy fiscal position, primarily for strategic purposes, which is what China is doing (e.g. Herrero and Alarcon 2012; Chang 2013).

Huge surpluses usually offer enormous choices to investors, and they might invest them foolishly, as many German banks have done during the housing bubble (OECD 2010, 88). But their harm is mainly financial. For consumers there is also the apparent choice of whether to replace a car every four years or every six years insofar as they can afford it. But the crucial difference is that for most consumer purchases, the overwhelming majority of working-class consumers only have limited choices, and can be expected to use most of their disposable income for consumption based on economic necessity. It is for these working-class consumers primarily that austerity measures are harmful, because austerity usually involves cuts in social programs, which forces workers to shift their purchases to social necessities such as health care or otherwise go without it. This process is also known as "risk privatization" (Hacker 2004).

Another argument by the austerity supporters is that if the debt-to-GDP ratio becomes too high, then economic growth will be lowered, and lower growth often means that the debt can impossibly be repaid. The solution, therefore, has to be a debt brake, as German chancellor Merkel suggested (Czuczka 2011), which stipulates that the government has to consolidate the budget in the expectation that debt will be lowered and economic recovery will come about. This was the line of reasoning that was used by the economists Reinhart and Rogoff (2010), who both argued that growth rates are very low, when the debt-to-GDP ratio is 90% or above. This hypothesis has been soundly debunked by economics graduate student, Thomas Herndon and his two co-authors (Herndon, Ash and Pollin 2013), who had discovered an Excel spreadsheet error in Reinhart and Rogoff's calculation, thus exaggerating the growth-depressing impacts of a high debt-to-GDP ratio.[45]

It stands to reason that a high debt-to-GDP ratio will not always pose an economic catastrophe if there are powerful other countries that can backstop the debts of debtor countries, such as the EU provides for Greece, or if the debts are owed to domestic financial institutions, companies and depositors, who have no interest to blackmail their own government with high rates of interest on government bonds, such as in Japan (where debt is expected to hit 230% of GDP in 2014- Riley 2013). These are not long-term solutions, and both Greece and Japan are facing hard choices with regard to their debt load, but it would be inaccurate to stick to an arbitrary debt-to-GDP ratio to interpret consequences on GDP growth. Furthermore, the policy implication for a high debt load, namely austerity and fiscal consolidation, provide no cover for sustained economic growth,

---

45 Herndon (2013) writes in a rebuttal to Reinhart and Rogoff's response (Reinhart and Rogoff 2013), "We [Herndon, Ash and Pollin] show that, contrary to R& R [Reinhart and Rogoff], there is no definitive threshold for the public debt/GDP ratio, beyond which countries will invariably suffer a major decline in GDP growth. The implication for policy is that, under particular circumstances, public debt can play a key role in overcoming a recession. The current historical moment, with historically high rates of mass unemployment in both the U.S. and Europe and with interest rates on U.S. Treasury bonds at historic lows, is precisely the set of circumstances under which we would expect public borrowing to have large positive effects, with comparably fewer costs. Moreover, it is precisely the set of circumstances under which we expect austerity to have substantial negative effects."

but imply more contraction and even more unsustainable debt loads amid greater social suffering.[46] In the next chapter, I examine the parties that want to maintain and defend the status quo.

---

46 In an interview with CNN, Mark Blyth explained very eloquently what austerity means to economic growth, "[T]ake a country, a typical European country has got an 80 percent debt-to-GDP ratio. Turn that into a fraction, 4 over 5. Now, hack away at, say, half of government expenditure, which is 40 percent of the economy. You've just taken 4 over 5 and turned it into 4 over 4. You've basically taken a 0.8 and turned it into a 1. So, you've now increased the amount of debt you have relative to the size of the economy." (CNN 2013)

Chapter 10: The Eurozone Crisis and the Power of Financiers and Germany

If austerity is such an economic and social failure in Europe, then it begs the question which interests want to pursue more austerity measures, and induce more pain and suffering among taxpayers, working and middle class people and the poor. I will first address the question how some European states were pushed into austerity policies. This analysis will largely apply to Greece, Spain, Portugal, Italy, Ireland and Cyprus. It has limited application to Latvia, and no application to the UK.[47]

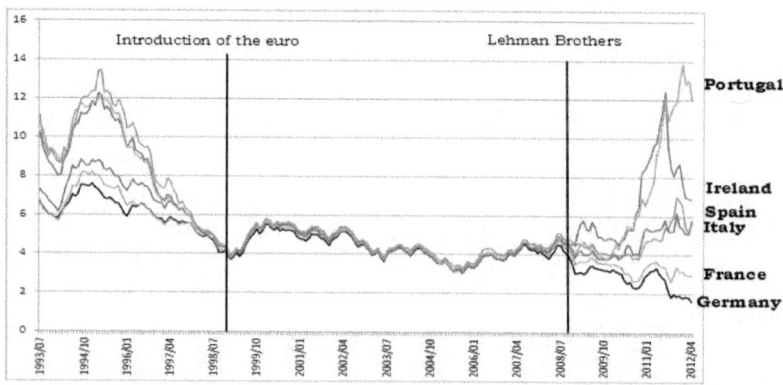

Illustration 32: Interest Rates on 10-Year Government Bonds in Various Eurozone Countries

The main constraining factor in the policy-making process of the peripheral eurozone countries is, in effect, their membership in the eurozone. The euro currency had been introduced in 1999 with the broad support of the governments in Europe. Countries like Greece or Italy were extremely thrilled about the accession into the eurozone, because their huge government debts which previously led to high interest rates on government bonds (as risk premium) were now more sustainable with the entry into the

---

47 For Latvia, not a member of the eurozone, the eurozone analysis applies, because they committed to fiscal austerity to join the eurozone. The UK is not part of the eurozone, and does not intend to be part of it. Its austerity policy did not happen under external duress.

eurozone. The interest rates for the government bonds declined to an average of 4-5% between 1999 and 2009 (cf. Illustration 32), which allowed the peripheral countries with weaker economies to increase their borrowing without fear of higher interest rates. The public debts of Greece, Portugal and Italy continued to increase in order to bankroll more consumption. Countries like Spain and Ireland abstained from greater public-sector debt, but allowed their deregulated banks to bankroll an expansion of the credit economy to stimulate investment in the housing market (Lapavitsas et al. 2010).

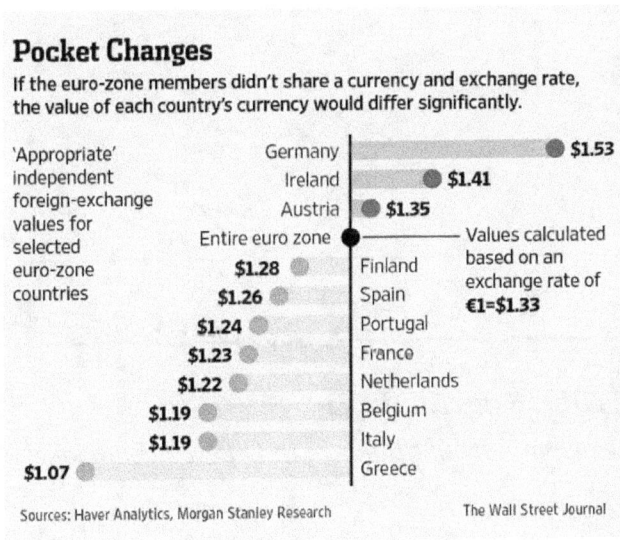

Illustration 33: Exchange Rate of Euro against the Dollar for Different Euro Countries

The euro really was a currency peg of the weaker, peripheral member states (Greece, Ireland, Italy, Portugal and Spain) to the stronger, core states (Germany, Netherlands, Austria, Finland and France). The strong states under the leadership of Germany insisted on low-inflation policies, corresponding to the German bad memory of hyperinflation in the 1920s and their export needs, which favors an undervalued currency on behalf of Germany. Illustration 33 shows that for some countries like Germany, Ireland or Austria the euro undervalues their currency, while for other countries like Spain, Portugal, Italy or Greece, the euro overvalues their currency. The unilateral monetary union, which was not coupled by a common, fiscal policy, proved to be an enormous moral hazard, because the peripheral countries borrowed huge quantities of capital which could never be repaid.

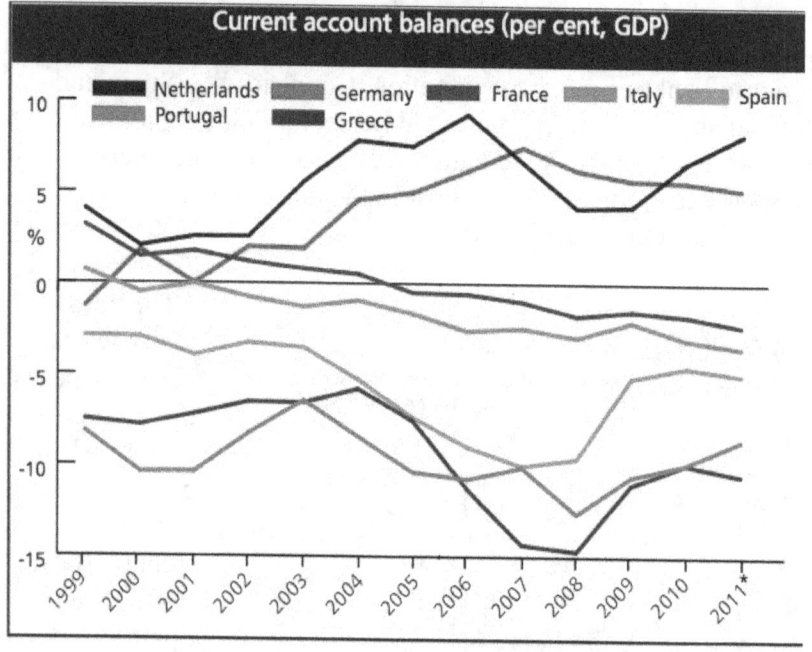

January-June 2011. Source: OECD

Illustration 34: Current Account Balance in Different Eurozone Countries

The investors, mainly the banks from the wealthy member states, used their excess capital to loan it to the peripheral countries, which not only fueled a housing boom, but underwrote the export-led boom of countries like Germany or Netherlands. The peripheral countries imported more, and the core countries exported more. The growing imbalance within the eurozone is best reflected in a comparison of the current account balances of the eurozone countries, showing that Germany and Netherlands were the net exporters, while Portugal, Spain, Italy, Greece and even France became the net importers (cf. Illustration 34). None of these imbalances would have mattered if the eurozone countries had accumulated enough political will to form a common fiscal union, and redistribute resources from the surplus countries to the deficit countries. But such an idea had never been seriously contemplated, and while the boom was happening it was difficult to warn the policy-makers about the negative effects of a monetary union without a fiscal union. The idea of a fiscal union is discussed in the next chapter.

With the great crash in 2008, the interconnected banking system immediately faced a liquidity and solvency crisis. All European governments stepped into the picture, and bailed out the stressed out banking system. Enormous amounts of private debt were converted into public debt. Even countries with relatively healthy public balance sheets, such as Ireland or Spain, when facing the obligations to their too-big-to-fail (and in some instances too-big-to-bail) banks, had their national debts sky-rocket after the bailouts had been orchestrated. The European Central Bank also stepped into the picture by guaranteeing to all banks the liquidity which they needed to stay intact. The ECB and other major central banks, such as the US Federal Reserve, the UK Bank of England and the Bank of Japan, cut the interest rates at the end of 2008 to currently less than 1% (cf. Illustration 35). The ECB cut the interest rate to 0.5% as of May 2013. These measures helped the banks to secure financing to stay intact, even as borrowing in the real economy remained weak and investments remained low.

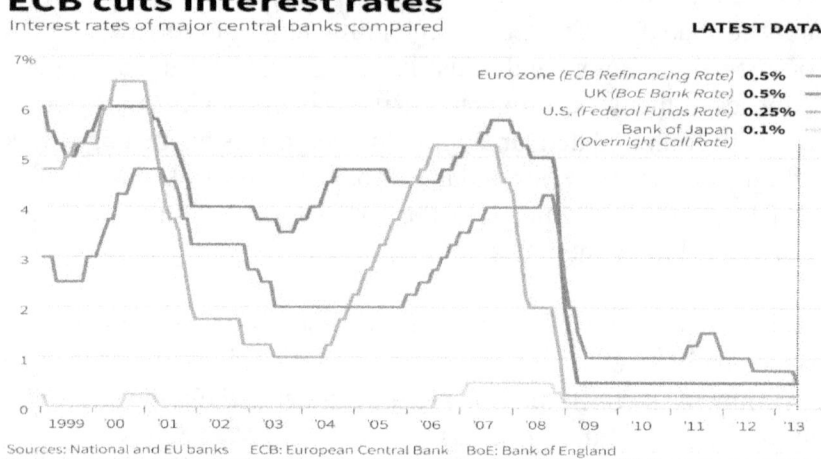

Illustration 35: Interest Rate of the Central Banks

For the core eurozone countries the bailouts were expensive, but affordable. For the peripheral countries, the burden of the bailout, the burden of interest rate hikes for government bonds, and the burden of the spreading recession, the greater jobless and benefit claims, and the shrinking tax revenues became unsustainable. The banking crisis was transformed into a sovereign debt crisis. Speculators and investors hit on the peripheral eurozone countries' debts and induced an increase in the interest rate on government bonds.

Who bails out the sovereign? Multiple round of bailouts from the core to the peripheral countries were implemented. These measures were called ESFS (European Stabilization Facility) and EFSM (European Financial Stabilization Mechanism). The IMF also added bailout funds. According to a March 2012 estimate, the total cost of the bailouts was €2 trillion (Herbert, Kloss and Borromeo 2012; also cf. Illustration 36). All these bailouts were handed out to the peripheral countries in exchange for fiscal consolidation or austerity measures. The hope was that with austerity measures the debts could be repaid and the economy might recover. But many people in the peripheral countries, who saw their pensions, wages and jobs eviscerated could not be fooled, and had realized that they were exploited to pay for the bank bailouts. The debts, in the mean time, could never be repaid via austerity, because the government played an important role in each of these afflicted economies. Reducing government expenditure meant reducing the overall size of the economy, which swelled the debt, and required further loans from the EU and the IMF, and more austerity and more anger among the population.

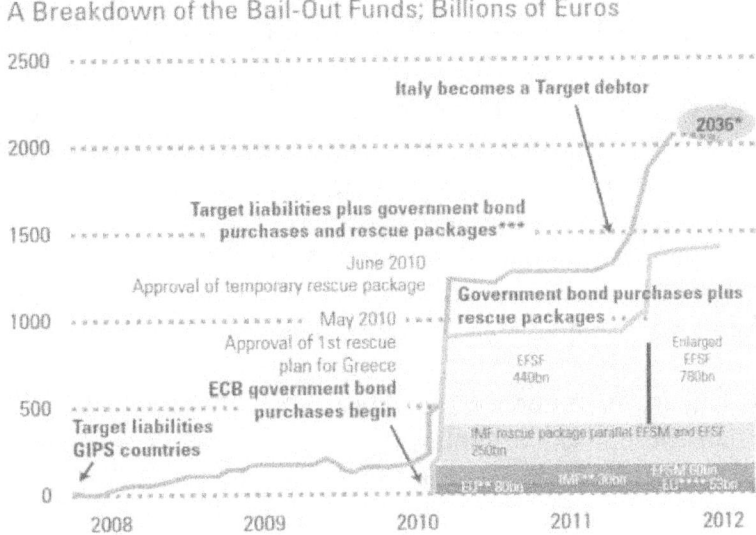

Illustration 36: Total Bailout Funds for Peripheral EU Countries

The interests of the investors and bankers, who wanted to see their losses minimized and their returns guaranteed, were preferred over the interests of the general public, who had to pay for the bailouts with austerity. So far creditors have lost money only in Greece, which had to write down its debt in 2012 or else face bankruptcy, but that is only a relatively small proportion of the total debt in the eurozone. Besides investors, Germany itself is also a powerful party, which could have played a more constructive role to resolve the eurozone crisis, but instead insisted on a continuation of the austerity policies across the continent. Instead of deploying its surplus to stimulate domestic demand or bankroll a European Marshall plan, German chancellor, Angela Merkel, insisted not only on austerity in the periphery, but also austerity in the core countries. Every European country should become like Germany. Every European country should become an export champion, which is utterly unrealistic.

In an interview, Merkel said that "Europe consists of little more than 7% of the world's population and generates 25% of global GDP, but it needs to finance 50% of all social spending, so it is obvious that it will have to work very hard to maintain its prosperity and its style of life" (Wharton 2013). In other words, Merkel doubts that the high social spending is still sustainable given the economic environment that Europe is in. That means that she wants to see even more austerity applied across Europe, since social programs are the biggest government expenditures in most countries in Europe. Merkel frequently referenced the importance of the peripheral eurozone countries to become more like a thrifty Swabian housewife (Euronews 2013).

On January 2013, the fiscal compact, a EU-treaty, which mandates strict fiscal discipline among EU members came into force (European Council 2013). It was spearheaded by the German government. In the same month, the German government succeeded in balancing its budget (DW 2013a). It wants other countries to do the same, even though it was Germany itself, which with its very competitive labor market policies had helped push the continent into a crisis. It was after the implementation of the "Agenda 2010" reform that Germany was able to expand its export sector with low-wage workers (Krebs and Scheffel 2013), and bring the uncompetitive peripheral countries into more debt (also discussed in Young and Semmler 2011, 9-11).

Illustration 37 shows the development of unit labor costs among several eurozone countries, and indicates that Germany held down wage increases, while wages in the periphery increased thanks to generous loan support (Lapavitsas et al. 2010; ILO 2012a, 46). Real monthly wages have been declining in Germany by -0.1% in the first quarter of 2013, after having seen some gains since 2010 (RWER Blog 2013). Germany had been the primary beneficiary of a common eurozone. But with further escalating debt burdens in the periphery and a shrinking export sector in Germany, the long-term interests of Germany has not been served with a continuing plea for more austerity.

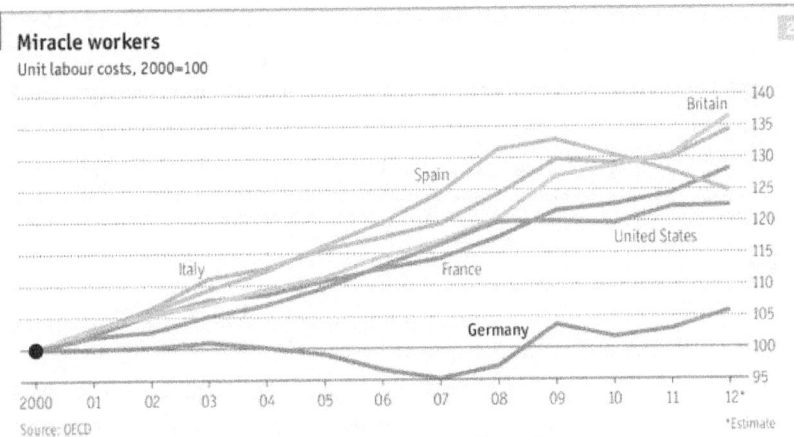

Illustration 37: Comparison of Unit Labor Costs

In the next chapter, I will discuss solutions and alternatives to the current austerity crisis.

Chapter 11: The Solution to the Crisis and the Alternatives to Austerity

In the mean time, the alternatives to austerity and more bailouts to delay the ever worsening problem were not really contemplated. The crisis harbors an opportunity, as a famous Chinese saying states, and there are different alternatives to what Europe could do to tackle its problems. The first alternative would be to have the debts canceled; the second to raise taxes on the wealthy rather than on the masses; the third is to dismantle the eurozone with currency devaluation; the fourth to have surplus countries like Germany raise domestic demand and apply financial aid directly to investment projects in the periphery ; the fifth is to create a fiscal union. I will discuss each of these possible solutions in further detail below.

1.Debt Cancellation
The first solution is to have the debts canceled via default. This step is currently the most important solution for the sovereign debt crisis in Europe. This has taken place in Greece, but it has done little to alleviate their debt problem, because the government debt-to-GDP ratio just decreased from 170.3% in 2011 to 156.9% in 2012.[48] This is far from sufficient to alleviate the burden of the Greek taxpayers, who are, in addition, struggling with a huge unemployment rate and a continuously shrinking economy. Greece is, therefore, not the ideal precedent for debt forgiveness.

A better example might be Iceland, which had developed an out-of-control banking sector, and a housing bubble since the late 1990s. After the 2008 collapse, the government had assumed enormous liabilities from the banking sector, and was faced with the choice between austerity and default. Iceland repudiated its debts after the financial crisis of 2008. The total loan amount forgiven is estimated to be 247.5 billion Icelandic krona (about $2

---

48 Trading Economics, "Greece Government Debt to GDP."
http://www.tradingeconomics.com/greece/government-debt-to-gdp

billion) (Margeirsson 2013). Iceland was fortunate enough to not be part of the eurozone. It owed a huge amount of debt to creditors, mainly British and Dutch banks. UK and Dutch government had sued Iceland to recover €4 billion in debts, which was soundly rejected by the Icelandic people in two referenda (BBC 2011). Iceland not only repudiated most of the debt, but also devalued its currency to ease exports rather than commit to a currency peg to the euro and austerity like many peripheral eurozone countries. Iceland's economic development turned positive in the beginning of 2011, though its GDP is still far away from the historical height in 2007.[49] Health conditions have improved in Iceland, because Iceland had defied IMF advice to reduce social spending, and instead raised spending in social protection. The local diet improved as McDonalds pulled out of Iceland, and people were cooking at home (mainly fish). Iceland also retained strict controls on alcohol (Karanikolos et al. 2013, 7).

The counter-argument of some investors, who will evidently lose their investments, is that if a country decides to repudiate the debt, then no more money will be lent to the defaulting countries. But this fear has not been substantiated. In June 2011, after being locked out of the bond market in late-2008, the Icelandic government started to sell new government bonds at about 5% interest rate to investors (Bases 2011). There is reason to believe that investors might be even more eager to purchase Icelandic bonds, because they know that the debt is more sustainably lower after default and the economy is recovering sufficiently to guarantee future repayment. The creditor wants the debtor on the hook, but the former has no interest in letting the latter starve. If this lesson were applied further across the continent, then better social and economic results might be obtained than what we currently witness.

---

49 Trading Economics, "Iceland GDP."
   http://www.tradingeconomics.com/iceland/gdp

Another counter-argument against default is that Iceland is merely a small country, and the sums that were lost in Iceland is negligible relative to the debt that Spain or Italy owes. A large default might be even costlier, and produce more economic turmoil. My response would be that the current crisis response, which involves bloodletting austerity policies, exacerbates the crisis even more, and an increase in social discontent helps the banking creditors while pushing the economy into a deeper depression. The investors when faced with losses via default may temporarily withdraw some capital out of Europe, but it is unthinkable that they would never ever lend any capital to a continent that consists of 25% of the global economy.

2. Wealth Tax

The second solution is to raise taxes on the wealthy, which is closely connected to the first solution. It is pretty evident that while wealthy creditors have an interest to extort more wealth out of the economies of Europe without accepting any default, they simultaneously hope to evade their responsibility to pay taxes to their governments.[50] The burden of debt, and the burden of social spending must be more broadly shared across society. But tax evasion and lobbying for less taxes is undermining the European tax base. One interesting example is Greece, where tax evasion is a chronic political problem. When the crisis broke out in Greece, €22 billion from 54,000 people exited the country before the tax hikes could take effect. The full cost of austerity was shouldered by the average workers in Greece.

In January 2009, French authorities had obtained the computer files of 2,000 wealthy Greek tax evaders, which the French finance minister, Christine Lagarde, had handed over to the Greek finance minister, George Papaconstantinou. Papaconstantinou in

---

50 Marx (1850) had argued that the French capitalists wanted the state to remain in a debt crisis, because the state debt was a source of speculation and personal enrichment, since they were the lenders of the state. Running state debts also allowed for subsidies from the government, which is reminiscent to the too-big-to-fail policy on banks in recent years.

turn handed the files over to the tax authority in the hope that the tax evaders would be investigated. But nobody in the ministry bothered to proceed with the prosecution, because the tax authorities were in the same boat with the tax evaders. When the Greek journalist, Kostas Vaxevanis, obtained a copy of the list, he published it immediately on his newspaper, and was imprisoned by the government. He faced trial for having leaked the information to the public, which he had regarded as his journalistic duty (Borger 2012).

Another famous example is the French actor, Gerard Depardieu, who upon the French government's announcement to raise marginal tax rates to 75% fled to Belgium and accepted Russian citizenship to lower his tax burden. He also took up residence in Russia's republic of Mordovia, and announced proudly in the ceremony, in which he was awarded Russian citizenship, "Glory to Russia, glory to Mordovia! This region doesn't have oil or gas but has rich people who make their wishes come true in life" (Amos 2013). Ingvar Kamprad, the founder of IKEA and one of the wealthiest men in Europe, on the other hand, returned to Sweden after a 40-year exodus in Switzerland. He had moved out of Sweden in the 1970s in order to protest the high-tax state. But since the new conservative government in Sweden had abolished a wealth tax, lowered income taxes and cut social spending, he was willing to return to his old home country (Trotman 2013).

Tax evasion is a pervasive problem in Europe. But some people might object that taxing the rich is not enough to pay off debts. But I find this objection not sustainable. It is estimated that the EU is losing €1 trillion annually in tax revenues due to tax evasion, even though the budget deficit of the EU-27 states was only €514 billion (Debating Europe 2013). One report reveals that an estimated $21-32 trillion is hidden in tax shelters (Henry 2012).

Others might object that the crisis in Europe does not contain a class content, because after all the economy as a whole is in a mess and the burden of adjustment must be carried by all alike. To that I would respond that most of the crisis costs have been carried by non-wealthy people in the form of income and sales tax increases, while social benefits such as pensions or health care, on which the rich do not depend on but the poor and middle class very much so, have been reduced. The bailout guarantees for the banks also reveals that the creditors, who are mostly wealthy, have received an endless insurance policy for their reckless gambling before and after the crisis. One report shows that the combined fortunes of people worth over $30 million in Germany, Switzerland, France and Italy had surged by 13% in 2012 to reach $3.4 trillion.

With more globalization at hand, the fortune of the wealthy people in Europe is becoming increasingly disconnected from the fortunes of the rest of the Europeans and the countries in which they reside. Amancio Ortega, for example, the founder of the Spanish clothing chain Zara, had increased his net worth by more than $10 billion in 2012 to more than $50 billion, while the Spanish economy is suffering from continued austerity and recession (Frank 2013). If Europe has an interest to maintain social cohesion and solve its economic travails it has to restrict the level of economic inequality (Wilkinson and Pickett 2010; Stiglitz 2012).

3. Dismantle the eurozone
The third solution is to dismantle the eurozone and the euro as a currency, and allow the weaker states to devalue their currency. There has been no precedent, thus far, for the abolition of a currency involving such a large part of the global economy. Some groups, such as the newly founded Alternative for Germany Party is calling for the abolition of the euro. It has received 7,000 membership applications so far (DW 2013b). Some economic analysts claim that a breakdown of the euro would imply a severe shrinkage of the economies in Europe (Rapoza 2012). Banks

would fail as they re-convert their balance sheets into the new weaker currency (Böll 2013). Costs for imports would rise dramatically, implying a fall in real wages and living standards. But aside from the immediate consequences, the peripheral economies in Europe are reasoning that with the re-introduction of their old currencies they are allowed to inflate their currency and repay the debt at a steep discount, since the real value of their currency will decline dramatically. A currency devaluation may mean that it will become more complicated again for countries like Greece or Italy to borrow money in the bond market, because the interest rates will be higher. It will also mean that their imports will be restricted due to a smaller purchasing power of their currency.

On the other hand, reclaiming sovereignty over their currency will make it more difficult for foreign entities such as the EU or the IMF to dictate harsh austerity policies that do not help their economies and trap the countries in a downward spiral. The largest objector to the abolition of the euro will certainly be Germany, because it has tremendously benefited from the single currency. Its very competitive exports would have strengthened the value of the German currency so strongly that their exports might decline. With the help of the euro, the single currency has undervalued the German currency and propelled the export sector. Germany will soon be forced to take a stance with regard to the continuing existence of the euro, because maintaining the apparently favorable status quo is backfiring due to ever greater bailout commitments from the German taxpayers.

While I think that breaking apart the eurozone is not the best of all solutions due to the high economic costs that is involved in the transition process, when the old currencies are brought back to the countries, this solution is to be preferred over the current commitment to austerity, which is pushing the day of decision into the future while more pain is inflicted on the people. Besides, under the given arrangements the eurozone countries are experiencing depressing economic growth.

A similar solution to the breakup of the euro would be a separation into two currency unions: the strong creditor countries, such as Austria, Netherlands, Finland and Germany would share a currency (Hutchinson 2011), and the deficit countries would form their own currency union and inflate that currency to improve their economy. Or at least Germany should leave the currency union, which would by itself devalue the euro (Sivy 2012). This would similarly be a viable solution, and does not go as far as re-creating 20 currencies. This solution does not necessarily address the long-term common governance issue, but it would make governance easier.

4. Increase Investments
The fourth solution is that the surplus-generating countries in the northern part of Europe should relieve the burdened countries in the south by increasing investments to stimulate domestic demand and to encourage economic development in the periphery. Realizing this option is a matter of political will, and the surplus-producing countries like Germany have very little inclination to raise domestic demand given their proclivity to exports and their relatively docile workforce, which had accepted a stagnation in real wages in exchange for greater export competitiveness and a guarantee of jobs.

The surplus countries should also contribute to the re-balancing of the different countries with a well-coordinated investment program, or a new Marshall plan, which strengthens the economies of the European periphery, creates jobs and relieves some of the social discontent that had been brewing as a result of the austerity programs. It is important for the peripheral countries to improve their export by raising the quality of their products (Simonazzi, Ginzburg and Nocella 2013). The peripheral countries would certainly like to see a rekindling of their economies with more investments, but they are not in the driver's seat with regard to this question. They should push for more subsidies on the European level.

The objection to such a Keynesian stimulus program is usually that the stimulus plan only has short-term benefits, and after the stimulus is over, no more lasting benefits exist. I would question the premise of those that make such argument, because they assume that whatever investment the government makes is wasted, because the investments are better left to the the private-sector, private capitalists. This premise is, of course, false. Government investments in education, infrastructure, telecommunication and health care are vital for any economy. The provision of crucial public goods contains inherent long-term benefits, which is denied by the critics of Keynesian stimulus. Another argument is that it is difficult to improve the economic fate of countries, that have long running economic disadvantages. How likely is it that all southern European countries can reach the same level of competitiveness as in Germany or in Austria? This is, indeed, a long-term challenge, and a leveling in living standards and productivity is no easy task, but it is socially and politically more responsible than a blind commitment to the status quo of austerity.

5. Fiscal Union

The fifth solution involves the potential creation of a real, fiscal union. In this proposal, the monetary union is complemented by a political union, in which fiscal decisions are made on a trans-European level. The structural, competitive weaknesses of the peripheral eurozone countries would have not been exploited with the provision of loans and a debt bubble, but by automatic fiscal transfers from the rich states to the poor states, similar to the US fiscal union. Rich states like New York or California constantly transfer funds to poor states like Tennessee or Mississippi. It would similarly work between Germany and Greece (cf. Illustration 38). The advantage of this political solution is that the euro currency can be retained and the difficult adjustment of raising productivity and marketability of the peripheral countries is not urgently necessary.

But this solution is understandably a hard sell among the wealthy countries in Europe, even though on behalf of social peace it is the most viable solution. Besides, it is not completely true that the net contributors to the fiscal union will not benefit, because, as I said, the monetary union had provided the markets for the surplus countries. Europe has some experience with a transfer union. The regional aid fund, which makes up about one-third of the total EU budget, is a transfer of funds from the wealthy regions of Europe to the poorer regions, even as the scope of the funds are rather limited (the EU budget is about 1% of the continent's GDP). Illustration 39 shows the beneficiary regions of regional aid shaded in red, and net contributing regions in blue.

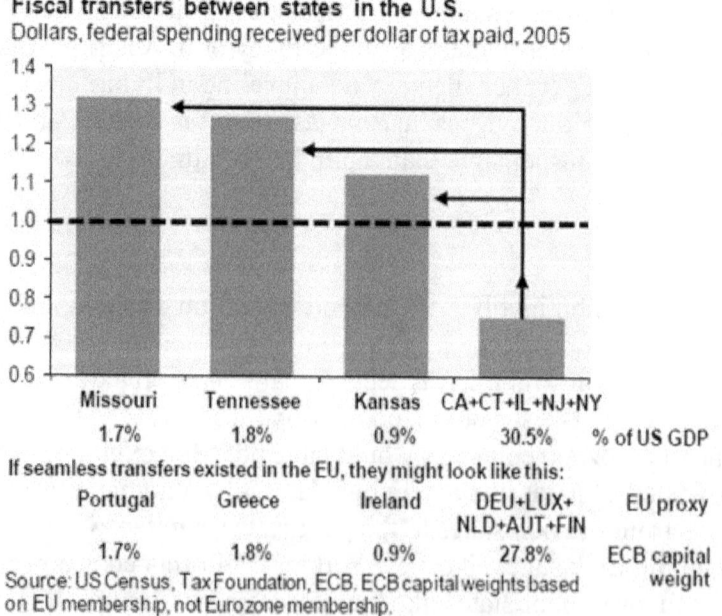

Illustration 38: Fiscal Transfers in the U.S.

In the mean time, the political wrangling continues, as the Germans are essentially unwilling to assume the debts of the peripheral eurozone countries. The West Germans have been haunted from the days of reunification with East Germany, which had imposed enormous transfer costs on the wealthier West Germany. There is little appetite for the assumption of common debt, even in the form of euro-bonds. The Greeks, who had been humiliated by crushing austerity measures, are, furthermore, psychologically unwilling to accept the dictates from Germany, which would inevitably happen with more fiscal authority residing in Brussels. The net contributor will have the most say.

Illustration 39: European Regional Development Fund 2007-13

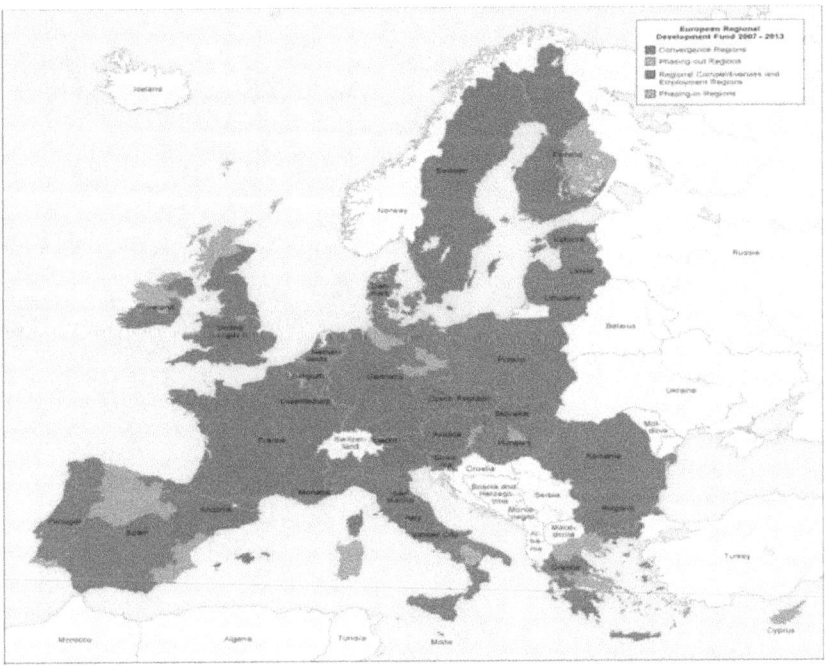

However, Germany emerged as the "unwilling hegemon" of Europe (Krönig 2013). It is a hegemon based on its economic strength, and unwilling because of its inward-looking history and dark memories of national socialism. The German sociologist, Ulrich Beck, goes as far as saying that Germany is an "accidental empire", which is economically powerful, but has no willingness to lead Europe in a different direction (Beck 2013). It is, therefore, unlikely to assume that Germany will abuse its economic strength. My objection to the fear of the weak countries is that the participation of those peripheral countries in the European governing process allows them to have their input voiced, and not the dictates of Germany, which is very reluctant to assert too much hard power anyway. The major drawback, of course, is that precisely because of Germany's lack to assertiveness, it remains stuck in the status quo rather than use political capital to advocate for a fiscal union.

Chapter 12: Conclusion

The political, social and economic consequences of austerity policies have been very severe. The main driver behind this austerity has been the continuing recession, the bailout of the banks, the huge government debt in many European countries, especially the peripheral countries, the insistence of the EU and IMF to balance the budget rather than to stimulate the economy, and the peculiar political-economic framework in the form of the eurozone. With every reduction in government spending and with every tax increase, the government has removed purchasing power out of the economy, making the economy smaller and the fiscal deficits and debt larger and not smaller. Every government that carried out austerity- either under duress like Greece, Spain, Portugal or Cyprus, or voluntarily as in the case of UK and Latvia- was not able to meet its intended fiscal target, because all the budget projections assumed that the economy would grow or at least not change without taking into consideration the economic ripple effects of austerity.

Besides the economic consequences of economic contraction and rising unemployment, there have been enormously negative social consequences to austerity: suicide and depression rates are on the rise; poverty and homelessness are increasing; health and educational services are deteriorating; and social unrest has become more common, while democratic legitimacy is undermined. Working, middle and lower class people are seeing their jobs and pensions disappear, while banks and creditors are continuously bailed out. It is in the interest of European policy-makers to consider an alternative direction to the current austerity policies in order to realize a more democratic and social Europe.

Postscript, October 2014

The manuscript on austerity policies in Europe was written during the summer of 2013, and was completed in July (largely in the Van Pelt library of the University of Pennsylvania). Since that time, the fundamental trends with respect to the rising levels of unemployment, inequality and poverty resulting from austerity measures have not really changed. Germany, serving as the EU's paymaster is still very much unwilling to massively increase investments in order to ameliorate the depressed economic situation, citing the need for fiscal restraint to balance the budget despite the contracting effects of such a policy. Internal devaluation in the form of lower wages and prices have remained the major form of adjustment.

Observing some of the current trends in France, where- despite a socialist party leadership- new austerity pledges are coming out to satisfy Berlin, one could fear that austerity has become the permanent wisdom in the EU. On the other hand, the election of the social democrat Matteo Renzi in Italy and Stefan Löfven in Sweden, and anti-austerity protests in France and other parts of Europe point to the possibility of swinging the political mood toward a more interventionist direction. By the latest, after the EU parliamentary elections in May 2014, we can see that the European electorate is very upset about the current political configuration, prioritizing deficit reduction targets over employment and the welfare state. The EU elections have brought numerous Euroskeptic parties to power, receiving one-quarter of the total vote.

The official tenor has been that European voters simply reject EU bureaucrats in Brussels taking more responsibilities away from national governments, and imposing unnecessary regulations like setting the shape and size of cucumbers that can be bought and sold. But the disappointment with the EU institutions also needs to be analyzed in the context of the current austerity policies that decrease the economic well-being of the electorate. It is the right-wing parties that blame immigrants and foreigners that can give a simple answer to the people, and use people's frustration about the political and economic situation to attack the ruling parties without offering any genuine solutions to the austerity crisis afflicting the whole continent. Even worse, by focusing on bashing immigrants or Muslims, they incite hatred and potentially violence, leading to even more social tensions.

Changing the course of economic policy principally requires a change in political attitudes and a change in the public discourse. At a time, when many people are confronted with less income and economic security, it becomes all the more important to stay educated about what the real problems are that are facing Europe. I have no doubt that with the austerity crisis intensifying, more people out on the street doing protests and opting for alternative parties during elections that new solutions will have to be discussed rather than the common wisdom, which has made lives harder for most people. If my book has contributed a little toward a greater understanding of austerity and its implications, then I have accomplished my goal.

References

Adams, Stephen. 2011. "NHS 'among Best Health Care Systems in the World'." *Telegraph*, November 9. http://www.telegraph.co.uk/health/healthnews/8877412/NHS-among-best-health-care-systems-in-the-world.html

Adomaitis, Nerijus, and Mia Shanley. 2011. "Latvia Teaches Austerity Pain and Gain to Greece." *Reuters*, September 23. http://www.reuters.com/article/2011/09/23/us-latvia-greece-austerity-idUSTRE78M28N20110923

Agnoletto, Stefano. 2012. "Italy: Austerity and Resistance." *Socialist Worker*, January 4. http://socialistworkercanada.com/2012/01/04/italy-austerity-and-resistance/

Alderman, Liz. 2010. "In Ireland, a Picture of the High Cost of Austerity." *New York Times*, June 28. http://www.nytimes.com/2010/06/29/business/global/29austerity.html?pagewanted=all

Alderman, Liz. 2013. "Cypriots Feel Betrayed by European Union." *New York Times*, April 1. http://www.nytimes.com/2013/04/02/business/global/cypriot-middle-class-feels-betrayed-by-europe-union.html?pagewanted=all&_r=0

Aldrick, Philip. 2011. "Chancellor Vows No Compromise on Cuts Despite Weak Growth." *Telegraph*, July 26. http://www.telegraph.co.uk/finance/economics/8663991/Chancellor-vows-no-compromise-on-cuts-despite-weak-growth.html

Alesina, Alberto, and Silvia Ardagna. 1998. "Tales of Fiscal Adjustments." *Economic Policy* 13(27): 489–545. http://dash.harvard.edu/bitstream/handle/1/2579822/Ardagna_TalesFiscal.pdf?sequence=2

Alesina, Alberto, and Silvia Ardagna. 2010. "Large Changes in Fiscal Policy: Taxes Versus Spending." In *Tax Policy and the Economy, Volume 24*, edited by Jeffrey R. Brown. Chicago:University of Chicago Press. http://www.nber.org/chapters/c11970.pdf

Alesina, Alberto, and Roberto Perotti. 1995. "Fiscal Expansions and Fiscal Adjustments in OECD Countries." *National Bureau of Economic Research*, Working Paper No. 5214. http://www.nber.org/papers/w5214

Alesina, Alberto, and Roberto Perotti. 1997. "Fiscal Adjustments in OECD Countries: Composition and Macroeconomic Effects." *IMF Staff Papers* 44(2):210-248.

Al Jazeera. 2012. "Spain: The Social Cost of Austerity." July 15. http://www.aljazeera.com/programmes/countingthecost/2012/07/201271412170352327.html

Al Jazeera. 2013a. "Thousands Protest over Spain Education Cuts." May 10. http://www.aljazeera.com/news/europe/2013/05/201359192955857931.html

Al Jazeera. 2013b. "Thousands Protest against Austerity in Italy." May 18. http://www.aljazeera.com/news/europe/2013/05/2013518182935218908.html

Almeida, Henrique and Anabela Reis. 2012. "Portugal's Budget Amendment Adds No New Austerity Measures." *Businessweek*, March 29. http://www.businessweek.com/news/2012-03-29/portugal-s-budget-amendment-adds-no-new-austerity-measures

Amos, Howard. 2013. "Gerard Depardieu Registered as Russian Resident amid Tax Row with France." *Guardian*, February 24. http://www.guardian.co.uk/film/2013/feb/24/gerard-depardieu-russian-resident-france

ANSAmed. 2013. "260,000 Children under 16 Put to Work in Italy." June 11. http://www.ansamed.info/ansamed/en/news/nations/italy/2013/06/11/260-000-children-16-put-work-Italy_8853552.html

Arens, Marianne. 2010. "Italian Students Protest University Austerity Legislation." *World Socialist Web Site*, December 28. http://www.wsws.org/en/articles/2010/12/ital-d28.html

Arens, Marianne. 2012. "Italian Prime Minister to Cut Additional €26 Billion." *World Socialist Web Site*, July 10. http://www.wsws.org/en/articles/2012/07/ital-j10.html

Arestis, Philip, and Theodore Pelagidis. 2010. "Absurd Austerity Policies in Europe." *Challenge* 53(6):54-61. http://courses.umass.edu/econ711-rpollin/Arestis--Absurd%20Austerity%20Policies%20in%20Europe.pdf

Aslund, Anders. 2012. "Southern Europe Ignores Lessons from Latvia at Its Peril." *Peterson Institute for International Economics*, Policy Brief: 12-17. http://www.piie.com/publications/pb/pb12-17.pdf

Aslund, Anders, and Valdis Dombrovskis. 2011. *How Latvia Came Through the Financial Crisis*. Washington, DC: Peterson Institute for International Economics.

Babones, Salvatore. 2012. "Income Inequality Undermines Economic Growth." *Latvian Institute of International Affairs*. http://liia.lv/en/blogs/income-inequality-undermines-economic-growth/

Balzli, Beat. 2010. "Greek Debt Crisis: How Goldman Sachs Helped Greece to Mask Its True Debt." *Spiegel International*, February 8. http://www.spiegel.de/international/europe/greek-debt-crisis-how-goldman-sachs-helped-greece-to-mask-its-true-debt-a-676634.html

Bandow, Doug. 2013. "The Triumph of Good Economics: 'Austere' Baltic States Outgrow their European Neighbor." *Cato Institute*, April 15. http://www.cato.org/publications/commentary/triumph-good-

economics-austere-baltic-states-outgrow-their-european?
utm_source=feedburner&utm_medium=feed&utm_campaign=Feed
%3A+CatoRecentOpeds+(Cato+Recent+Op-eds

Bases, Daniel. 2011. "Investors Buy into Iceland and Latvia Debt Issues." *Reuters*, June 9. http://www.reuters.com/article/2011/06/09/markets-bonds-iceland-idUSN09186989201106099

BBC. 2009a. "Small Business Loan Plan Unveiled." *British Broadcasting Corporation*, January 14. http://news.bbc.co.uk/2/hi/business/7827273.stm

BBC. 2009b. "At-a-Glance: Budget 2009." *British Broadcasting Corporation*, April 22. http://news.bbc.co.uk/2/hi/uk_news/politics/8011882.stm

BBC. 2009c. "Pre-Budget Report Sees Darling Raise National Insurance." *British Broadcasting Corporation*, December 9. http://news.bbc.co.uk/2/hi/uk_news/politics/8402769.stm

BBC. 2010a. "George Osborne Outlines Detail of £6.2bn Spending Cuts." *British Broadcasting Corporation*, May 24. http://news.bbc.co.uk/2/hi/uk_news/politics/8699522.stm

BBC. 2010b. "Italy Joins Euro Austerity Drive." *British Broadcasting Corporation*, May 25. http://www.bbc.co.uk/news/10157432

BBC. 2010c. "Budget: Osborne's 'Tough' Package Puts VAT up to 20%." *British Broadcasting Corporation*, June 22. http://www.bbc.co.uk/news/10371590

BBC. 2010d. "Quango List Shows 192 to be Axed." *British Broadcasting Corporation*, October 14. http://www.bbc.co.uk/news/uk-politics-11538534

BBC. 2010e. "Spending Review 2010: Key Points at-a-Glance." *British Broadcasting Corporation*, October 21. http://www.bbc.co.uk/news/uk-politics-11569160

BBC. 2011. "UK and Netherlands to Sue Iceland over Lost Deposits." *British Broadcasting Corporation*, April 10. http://www.bbc.co.uk/news/business-13029210

BBC. 2012a. "Spain Budget Imposes Further Austerity Measures." *British Broadcasting Corporation*, September 27. http://www.bbc.co.uk/news/business-19733995

BBC. 2012b. "Portugal Passes Another Austerity Budget." *British Broadcasting Corporation*, November 27. http://www.bbc.co.uk/news/business-20513821

BBC. 2013a. "Eurozone Crisis: Portugal Protests against Austerity." *British Broadcasting Corporation*, March 2. http://www.bbc.co.uk/news/world-europe-21643853

BBC 2013b. "Portugal's Austerity Government Feels the Pinch." *British Broadcasting Corporation*, July 2. http://www.bbc.co.uk/news/world-europe-23154232

Beck, Ulrich. 2013. "Germany Has Created an Accidental Empire." *Social*

Europe Journal, March 25. http://www.social-europe.eu/2013/03/germany-has-created-an-accidental-empire/

Belvis, Antonio Giulio de, Francesca Ferre, Maria Lucia Specchia, Luca Vlerio, Giovanni Fattore, and Walter Ricciardi. 2012. "The Financial Crisis in Italy: Implications for the Healthcare Sector." *Health Policy* 106(1):10-16. http://www.sciencedirect.com/science/article/pii/S016885101200108X)

Benoit, Angeline. 2012. "EU Sees Spain's Budget Measures Failing to Tackle Deficit." *Businessweek*, November 7. http://www.businessweek.com/news/2012-11-07/eu-sees-spain-s-budget-measures-failing-to-tackle-deficit

Bergeijk, Peter A. G., Jarig van Sinderen, and Ben A. Vollaard. 1999. *Structural Reform in Open Economies: A Road to Success?* Glos, UK: Edward Elgar Publishing.

Blanchflower, David. 2012. "The Private Sector Isn't Picking up the Slack." *New Statesman*, March 16. http://www.newstatesman.com/economy/2012/03/private-sector-public-jobs

Blyth, Mark. 2013a. *Austerity: The History of a Dangerous Idea*. New York: Oxford University Press.

Blyth, Mark. 2013b. "Why Austerity Is a Dangerous Idea." *Time*, April 18. http://ideas.time.com/2013/04/18/why-austerity-is-a-dangerous-idea/

Blyth, Mark, and Jonathan Hopkin. 2010. "How the Flexible Labour Market Failed Europe." *Guardian*, May 20. http://www.guardian.co.uk/commentisfree/2010/may/20/italy-spain-debt-crisis-markets

Böll, Sven. 2013. "German 'Alternative': Parallel Currency Idea Carries Great Risks." *Spiegel International*, April 22. http://www.spiegel.de/international/business/economists-say-parallel-currencies-in-eurozone-would-fail-a-895731.html

Borger, Julian. 2012. "Greek Magazine Editor in Court for Naming Alleged Tax Evaders." *Guardian*, October 28. http://www.guardian.co.uk/world/2012/oct/28/greek-editor-court-tax-evaders

Bowcott, Owen. 2012. "First Squatter Jailed under New Law." *Guardian*, September 27. http://www.guardian.co.uk/society/2012/sep/27/first-squatter-jailed-new-law

Bridge, Robert. 2013. "Portugal to Lift Retirement Age, Working Hours in Austerity Drive." *Russia Today*, May 4. http://rt.com/business/portugal-austerity-protests-eurozone-810/

Bryan-Low, Cassell. 2012. "U.K.'s Conservatives Seek Further Austerity Measures." *Wall Street Journal*, October 7. http://online.wsj.com/article/SB10000872396390443615804578042 0

43634323094.html

Burke, Michael. 2012. "Ireland's 'Austerity' Is Working- for Profits." *Left Futures*, November 12. http://www.leftfutures.org/2012/11/irelands-austerity-is-working-for-profits/

Businessweek. 2010. "Portugal: Political Parties Clinch Austerity Deal." October 30. http://www.businessweek.com/ap/financialnews/D9J66Q700.htm

Butler, Patrick and Amelia Gentleman. 2013. "Benefit Cut Putting 200,000 Children in Poverty Must be Stopped, Experts Say." *Guardian*, March 27. http://www.guardian.co.uk/society/2013/mar/27/benefit-cuts-poverty-stopped-experts

Cala, Andres. 2011. "Voters Move Portugal to the Right amid Economic Frustrations." *Christian Science Monitor*, June 6.

Caldas, Jose Castro. 2012. "The Consequences of Austerity Policies in Portugal." *Friedrich Ebert Stiftung*, August. http://library.fes.de/pdf-files/id-moe/09311.pdf

Carrera, Leandro. 2012. "The Eurozone Crisis Has Accelerated the Reform of Public Pensions in Italy, But Future Pensions May No Longer Provide an Adequate Income in Retirement." *LSE Blogs*, November 2. http://blogs.lse.ac.uk/europpblog/2012/11/02/italy-pension-system/

Castle, Stephen. 2013. "Austerity Remains Key to Britain's Economic Plan." *New York Times*, June 26. http://www.nytimes.com/2013/06/27/world/europe/austerity-remains-key-to-britains-economic-plan.html?_r=0

Chang, Bao. 2013. "China to Invest More in Greece." *China Daily*, May 18. http://www.chinadaily.com.cn/cndy/2013-05/18/content_16508611.htm

Channel4. 2011. "Italy Austerity Package Passed." July 15. http://www.europeaninstitute.org/Special-G-20-Issue-on-Financial-Reform/austerity-measures-in-the-eu.html

Charalabidis, Yannis. 2011. "Greek Budget Visualization: Where Does the Money Go?" *Governance Transformation Blogspot*, June 23. http://t-government.blogspot.com/2011/06/greek-budget-visualisation-where-do.html

Charalambous, Lorys. 2012. "New Austerity Measures Approved in Cyprus." *Tax-News*, December 12. http://www.tax-news.com/news/new_austerity_measures_approved_in_cyprus____58720.html

Chaturvedi, Neelabh, Emese Bartha, and Eamon Quinn. 2012. "Irish Return to Bond Markets is Turning Point." *Wall Street Journal*, July 26. http://online.wsj.com/article/SB10000872396390443477104577550724270424592.html

Cheng, Maria. 2011. "Health-Care Cuts in Britain: Draconian?" *Christian Science Monitor*, December 11.

http://www.csmonitor.com/Business/Latest-News-Wires/2011/1211/Health-care-cuts-in-Britain-draconian

Chislett, William. 2013. *Spain: What Everyone Needs to Know*. New York: Oxford University Press.

Ciancio, Antonella. 2012. "Italy Debt Crisis Pushes More Than Half of Italians to Recycle Food." *Huffington Post*, October 19. http://www.huffingtonpost.com/2012/10/19/italy-debt-crisis_n_1984509.html

Clendenning, Alan. 2010. "Spain Approves New Austerity Measures, Limited Stimulus." *Huffington Post*, December 3. http://www.huffingtonpost.com/2010/12/03/spain-approves-new-austerity-measures_n_791964.html

CNBC. 2013. "Italy Youth Unemployment Hits Record 40.5%." May 31. http://www.cnbc.com/id/100779427

CNN. 2012. "Crowds Throng London in March against UK Austerity." *Cable News Network*, October 20. http://www.cnn.com/2012/10/20/world/europe/uk-anti-austerity-march

CNN. 2013. "Quest Means Business- Transcript." May 7. http://transcripts.cnn.com/TRANSCRIPTS/1305/07/qmb.01.html

Collignon, Stefan. 2013. "Austerity Versus Growth (I): Why We Can't Go On Like This." *Social Europe Journal*, April 29. http://www.social-europe.eu/2013/04/austerity-versus-growth-i-why-we-cant-go-on-like-this/

Collins, Joan. 2013. "Are We Proud that Ireland is the Poster Child of Austerity?" *Journal*, May 9. http://www.thejournal.ie/readme/ireland-poster-child-austerity-joan-collins-899403-May2013/

Coy, Peter. 2010. "Keynes vs. Alesina. Alesina Who?" *Businessweek*, June 29. http://www.businessweek.com/stories/2010-06-29/keynes-vs-dot-alesina-dot-alesina-who

Cyprus Lawyer. 2011. "Austerity Measures Approved." December 15. http://thecypruslawyer.com/the-austerity-measures-approved/cyprus

Cyprus Property News. 2012. "EU Congratulates Cyprus on Measures." January 24. http://www.news.cyprus-property-buyers.com/2012/01/24/eu-congratulates-cyprus-on-measures/id=0010451

Czuczka, Tony. 2011. "Merkel Says EU Creating Fiscal 'Debt Brake' for All Countries With Euro." *Bloomberg*, December 8. http://www.bloomberg.com/news/2011-12-09/merkel-says-eu-creating-fiscal-debt-brake-for-all-countries-with-euro.html

Davis, Carlo. 2013. "Cyprus Bailout Protests: Cypriots March against Bank Deal." *Huffington Post*, March 18. http://www.huffingtonpost.com/2013/03/18/cyprus-bailout-protests_n_2902406.html

Day, Paul, and Tomas Cobos. 2012. "Spain Protests Labor Reforms As Hundreds of Thousands Take to Streets." *Huffington Post*, February 19. http://www.huffingtonpost.com/2012/02/19/spain-protests-labor-reforms_n_1287491.html

Debating Europe. 2013. "Is Tax Evasion Making Europe's Crisis Worse?" July 1. http://www.debatingeurope.eu/2013/07/01/is-tax-evasion-making-the-crisis-worse/#.UecmuNZlS9t

Department of Finance. 2011. "Medium-Term Fiscal Statement." *Government of Ireland*. http://www.finance.gov.ie/documents/publications/presentation/Fiscalstat.pdf

Dowsett, Sonya. 2010. "Spain Austerity Plan Scrapes Through Parliament." *Reuters*, May 27. http://www.reuters.com/article/2010/05/27/us-spain-idUSTRE64Q54T20100527

Doyle, Dara. 2012. "Ireland's Exports Keep the Economy Afloat." *Businessweek*, November 15. http://www.businessweek.com/articles/2012-11-15/irelands-exports-keep-the-economy-afloat

Duthel, Heinz. 2010. *European Debt Crisis 2011*. IAC Society.

DW. 2013a. "Germany Marks Balanced Budget amid Crisis." *Deutsche Welle*, January 15. http://www.dw.de/germany-marks-balanced-budget-amid-crisis/a-16521827

DW. 2013b. "Alternative for Germany Party Calls for Abolition of Euro." *Deutsche Welle*, April 14. http://www.dw.de/alternative-for-germany-party-calls-for-abolition-of-euro/a-16742836

EBRD. 2012. "Vienna Initiative- Moving to a New Phase." *European Bank for Reconstruction and Development*, April. http://www.ebrd.com/downloads/research/factsheets/viennainitiative.pdf

Economist. 2009. "Hard Times." December 10. http://www.economist.com/node/15073973

Economist. 2010. "And for My Next Trick." November 4. http://www.economist.com/node/17421424

Economist. 2011. "The Midget and the Mighty." August 6. http://www.economist.com/node/21525458

Economist. 2013. "Through a Glass, Darkly." April 27. http://www.economist.com/news/finance-and-economics/21576666-outlook-even-grimmer-it-was-time-bail-out-through

Eglitis, Aaron. 2008. "Latvia Secures 7.5 Billion Euros in IMF, EU Loans." *Bloomberg*, December 19. http://www.bloomberg.com/apps/news?pid=newsarchive&sid=aGIcnXZNN1I4

Elliott, Larry. 2010. "Budget Will Cost 1.3M Jobs- Treasury." *Guardian*, June 29. http://www.guardian.co.uk/uk/2010/jun/29/budget-job-losses-unemployment-austerity

Elliott, Larry. 2011. "Ireland becomes Poster Child for Implementing Austerity Programmes." *Guardian*, November 27. http://www.guardian.co.uk/business/economics-blog/2011/nov/27/ireland-poster-child-for-austerity-programmes

Elyatt, Holly. 2013. "'Unfair, Dangerous' Cyprus Deal Whacks Rich Russians." *CNBC*, March 18. http://www.cnbc.com/id/100562036

Emmott, Robin. 2012. "Euro Zone Joblessness Risks 'Economic Disaster'." *Reuters*, October 1. http://www.reuters.com/article/2012/10/01/us-eurozone-unemployment-idUSBRE8900JQ20121001

Emsden, Christopher. 2012. "Italy Reneges on Vow to Balance 2013 Budget." *Wall Street Journal*, April 18. http://online.wsj.com/article/SB10001424052702303513404577351560527620108.html

ESU. 2013. "Education Should be Protected from Austerity." *European Students' Union*, April 9. http://www.esu-online.org/news/article/6001/Education-should-be-protected-from-austerity/

Eurobank. 2013. "Portugal: Labour Market Reforms- A Summary of Main Problems and Actions Taken." *Eurobank Research*, Focus Notes, June 13. http://www.eurobank.gr/Uploads/Reports/56_FOCUS_NOTES_PORTUGAL_LABOUR_MARKET_REFORMS.pdf

Euro Health Net. 2011. "Greece – Augmentation of 40% of Rate Suicide." September 25. http://eurohealthnet.eu/sites/eurohealthnet.eu/files/press-release/News%20suicide%20rate%20Greece%20-%20%2020111006.pdf

Euronews. 2012. "Italy's Anti-Austerity Protests Erupt into Violence." November 14. http://www.euronews.com/2012/11/14/italy-s-anti-austerity-protests-erupt-into-violence/

Euronews. 2013. "Merkel Ruft Jahre der schwäbischen Hausfrau aus." October 28. http://de.euronews.com/2011/10/28/merkel-ruft-jahre-der-schwaebischen-hausfrau-aus/

Euronomist. 2012. "Austerity Measures and Reforms in Cyprus." September 25. http://euronomist.blogspot.com/2012/09/austerity-measures-and-reforms-in-cyprus.html

European Commission. 2009. "Portfolio of Indicators for the Monitoring of the European Strategy for Social Protection and Social Inclusion." Employment, Social Affairs and Equal Opportunities DG Social Protection and Social Integration, Brussels.

European Commission. 2012. "Ireland's Economic Crisis: How Did It Happen and What Is Being Done about It?" June 12. http://ec.europa.eu/ireland/key-eu-policy-areas/economy/irelands-economic-crisis/index_en.htm

European Council. 2013. "'Fiscal Compact' Entered into Force on 1 January

2013." January 1. http://www.european-council.europa.eu/home-page/highlights/fiscal-compact-enters-into-force-on-1-january-2013?lang=en

Evans-Pritchard, Ambrose. 2008. "Ireland Leads Eurozone into Recession." *Telegraph*, September 25. http://www.telegraph.co.uk/finance/economics/3079522/Ireland-leads-eurozone-into-recession.html

Evans-Pritchard, Ambrose. 2013. "Italy Could Need EU Rescue Within Six Months, Warns Mediobanca." *Telegraph*, June 24. http://www.telegraph.co.uk/finance/economics/10139939/Italy-could-need-EU-rescue-within-six-months-warns-Mediobanca.html

EWN Business. 2011. "Spain's Latest Austerity Measures are Now in Force." January 11. http://www.ewnbusiness.com/442/spain%E2%80%99s-latest-austerity-measures-are-now-in-force

Eyraud, Luc, and Anke Weber. 2013. "The Challenge of Debt Reduction during Fiscal Consolidation." *International Monetary Fund*, Working Paper, No. 13/67. http://www.imf.org/external/pubs/ft/wp/2013/wp1367.pdf

FAZ. 2013. "Griechenland-Hilfe vor allem an Banken und Reiche." *Frankfurter Allgemeine Zeitung*, June 17. http://www.faz.net/aktuell/wirtschaft/europas-schuldenkrise/griechenland/europas-schuldenkrise-griechenland-hilfe-vor-allem-an-banken-und-reiche-12224468.html

Feigl, Georg. 2012. "Failing Austerity in Europe: The Case of Spain." *Social Europe Journal*, April 4. http://www.social-europe.eu/2012/04/failing-austerity-in-europe-the-case-of-spain/

Financial Mirror. 2011. "Cyprus Civil Servants Strike over Austerity Measures." December 14. http://www.financialmirror.com/news-details.php?nid=25244

Fitzpatrick, Richard. 2013. "The Body Economic: Why Austerity Kills." *Irish Examiner*, May 30. http://www.irishexaminer.com/lifestyle/features/humaninterest/the-body-economic-why-austerity-kills-232744.html

Fleming, Jeremy. 2012. "EU Health Forum Hears Alarm Bells over Budget Cuts, Inefficiencies." *EurActiv*, October 3. http://www.euractiv.com/specialreport-future-european-he/health-sector-change-perish-news-515141

Foley, Stephen. 2011. "What Price the New Democracy? Goldman Sachs Conquers Europe." *Independent*, November 18. http://www.independent.co.uk/news/business/analysis-and-features/what-price-the-new-democracy-goldman-sachs-conquers-europe-6264091.html

Fox, Benjamin. 2013. "Italy to Leave EU 'Crisis List' after Cutting Deficit." *EU Observer*, May 27. http://euobserver.com/economic/120263

France24. 2011. "Thousands Rally in Portugal to Protest Austerity Plans."

October 1. http://www.france24.com/en/20111001-thousands-rally-protest-austerity-plans-porto-lisbon-portugal-coelho
France24. 2012. "Portugal Unveils Harsh Austerity Budget." October 15. http://www.france24.com/en/20121015-portugal-submits-harsh-austerity-budget-financial-crisis-debt-euro-bail-out
Frank, Robert. 2013. "What Slowdown? Rich Europeans Only Getting Richer." *CNBC*, June 28. http://www.cnbc.com/id/100850397
Frankel, Jeffrey. 2013. "The Flawed Origins of Expansionary Austerity." *Project Syndicate*, May 20. http://www.project-syndicate.org/commentary/the-case-against-expansionary-austerity-by-jeffrey-frankel
Frayer, Lauren. 2012. "Tough Cuts in Portugal May be Exacting High Toll." *NPR*, April 13. http://www.npr.org/2012/04/13/150580358/tough-cuts-in-portugal-may-be-exacting-high-toll
Gallardo, Angels. 2012. "Las muertes por suicidio crecen el 10% en Catalunya durante la crisis." *El Periodico*, 23 June.
Gates, Sara. 2013. "Firefighters Clash with Riot Police in Spain during Austerity Protest." *Huffington Post*, May 29. http://www.huffingtonpost.com/2013/05/29/firefighters-riot-police-austerity-protest_n_3353851.html
Gestha. 2011. "Reducir El Fraude Fiscal Y La Economia Sumergida: Una Medida Vital E Imprescindible Para Superar La Crisis." *Sindicato de Tecnicos del Ministerio de Hacienda*, November 15. http://www.gestha.es/archivos/informacion/monograficos/2011/reducir-el-fraude-fiscal-y-la-economia-sumergida.pdf
Georgiopoulos, George, and Renee Maltezou. 2013. "Greek Youth Unemployment Rises Above 60 Percent." *Huffington Post*, May 9. http://www.huffingtonpost.com/2013/05/09/greek-youth-unemployment-_n_3244437.html
Georgiou, Georgios, and Paul Tugwell. 2013. "Cyprus Unemployed Rises 30% in May as Retail, Building Shrinks." *Bloomberg*, June 5. http://www.bloomberg.com/news/2013-06-05/cyprus-unemployed-rises-30-in-may-as-retail-building-shrinks.html
Ghost Agenda. 2013. "The Cypriot Financial Crisis Explained." March 28. http://ghostagenda.com/2013/03/28/the-cypriot-financial-crisis-explained/
Giavazzi, Francesco, and Marco Pagano. 1990. "Can Severe Fiscal Contractions Be Expansionary? Tales of Two European Countries." *National Bureau of Economic Research, Macroeconomics Annual* 5:75-111.
Giles, Chris, and Andrew Bounds. 2012. "Brutal for Britain." *The Financial Times*, January 15.
Giles, Ciaran, and Daniel Woolls. 2012. "Spain's Budget Cuts to Shave $80B in Wake of Euro Bailout." *Huffington Post*, July 11.

http://www.huffingtonpost.ca/2012/07/11/spain-budget-cuts-2012_n_1664009.html

Governo Italiono. 2012. "Towards a Flexible and Fair Labour Market in Italy." *Presidenza del Consiglio dei Ministri*, June 28. http://www.governo.it/Presidenza/Comunicati/dettaglio.asp?d=68570

Graham, Carol. 1998. *Private Markets for Public Goods: Raising the Stakes in Economic Reform*. Washington D.C.: Brookings Institution Press.

Guajardo, Jaime, Daniel Leigh and Andrea Pescatori. 2011. "Expansionary Austerity: New International Evidence." *IMF Working Paper*, No. 11/158. http://www.imf.org/external/pubs/ft/wp/2011/wp11158.pdf

Guillen, Mauro F., and Emilio Ontiveros. 2012. *Global Turning Points: Understanding the Challenges for Business in the 21st Century*. New York: Oxford University Press.

Gumbel, Peter. 2013. "Cyprus Rescue: The Destruction of a Tax Haven." *Time*, March 25. http://business.time.com/2013/03/25/cyprus-rescue-the-destruction-of-a-tax-haven/

Guttman, Amy. 2013. "In Italy, Austerity Is Served on Homemade Bread." *Atlantic*, May 17. http://www.theatlantic.com/international/archive/2013/05/in-italy-austerity-is-served-on-homemade-bread/275951/

Hacker, Jacob S. 2004. "Privatizing Risk without Privatizing the Welfare State: the Hidden Politics of Social Policy Retrenchment in the United States." *American Political Science Review* 98(2): 243-260.

Hall, James. 2012. "Bank of England Policymaker Enters 'Granny Tax' Debate." *Telegraph*, March 25. http://www.telegraph.co.uk/finance/budget/9165918/Bank-of-England-policymaker-enters-granny-tax-debate.html

Han, Xue. 2012. "The Journey of Austerity in Europe." *Global Infrastructure*, June. http://www.globalinfrastructurellc.com/storage/The%20Journey%20of%20Austerity%20in%20Europe%20-%20The%20Past%20Present%20and%20Future%20of%20EU's%20Debt%20Crisis%20and%20Austerity%20Paths.pdf

Hannon, Paul. 2011. "IMF Backs U.K. Spending Cuts." *Wall Street Journal*, June 7. http://online.wsj.com/article/SB10001424052702304432304576369223709373918.html

Harris, John. 2013. "The Bedroom Tax Has Made Huge Problems Even Worse." *Guardian*, June 9. http://www.guardian.co.uk/commentisfree/2013/jun/09/bedroom-tax-huge-problems-worse

Hatton, Barry. 2012. "Portugal's Woes Drive Personal Bankruptcies." *Businessweek*, March 28. http://www.businessweek.com/ap/2012-03/D9TPE5MO0.htm

Haughey, Nuala. 2010. "Irish Protest against Austerity Cuts." *National*,

November 28. http://www.thenational.ae/news/world/irish-protest-against-austerity-cuts

Heckle, Harold. 2012. "Spain Austerity Protests: Thousands March in Madrid." *Huffington Post*, October 13. http://www.huffingtonpost.com/2012/10/13/spain-austerity-protests_n_1963919.html

Henry, James S. 2012. "The Price of Offshore Revisited: New Estimates for the 'Missing' Global Private Wealth, Income, Inequality, and Lost Taxes." *Tax Justice Network*, July. http://www.taxjustice.net/cms/upload/pdf/Price_of_Offshore_Revisited_120722.pdf

Herbert, Gerhardt, Brian L. Kloss, and Regina G. Borromeo. 2012. "Global High Yield Perspectives." *Brandywine Global Investment Management LLC*, March 31. http://www.zerohedge.com/sites/default/files/images/user5/imageroot/2012/05-2/Brandywine%20Global%20Q1%202012.pdf

Herndon, Thomas. 2013. "The Grad Student Who Took Down Reinhard and Rogoff Explains Why They're Fundamentally Wrong." *Business Insider*, April 22. http://www.businessinsider.com/herndon-responds-to-reinhart-rogoff-2013-4

Herndon, Thomas, Michael Ash and Robert Pollin. 2013. "Does High Public Debt Consistently Stifle Economic Growth? A Critique of Reinhart and Rogoff." *Political Economy Research Institute*, Working Paper Series, No. 322. http://www.peri.umass.edu/fileadmin/pdf/working_papers/working_papers_301-350/WP322.pdf

Herrero, Isabel, and Jose M. Alarcon. 2012. "China's 'Going out' Investment in Spain." *HKTDC Research*, December 12. http://economists-pick-research.hktdc.com/business-news/article/International-Market-News/China-s-going-out-investment-in-Spain/imn/en/1/1X000000/1X09QRQ1.htm

Higgins, Andrew. 2013. "Used to Hardship, Latvia Accepts Austerity, and Its Pain Eases." *New York Times*, January 1. http://www.nytimes.com/2013/01/02/world/europe/used-to-hardship-latvia-accepts-austerity-and-its-pain-eases.html?pagewanted=all&_r=0

Homs, Daniel Bosque. 2013. "Spain's 'Lost Generation': Youth Unemployment Hits 57 Percent." *Huffington Post*, May 28. http://www.huffingtonpost.com/2013/05/28/spain-lost-generation_n_3344183.html

House of Commons. 2009. "Banking Crisis: Dealing with the Failure of the UK Banks." *Treasury Committee, Parliament of UK*, April 21. http://www.publications.parliament.uk/pa/cm200809/cmselect/cmtreasy/416/416.pdf

Hudson, Michael, and Jeffrey Sommers. 2012. "Why Latvia's Austerity Model Can't Be Exported." *New Economic Perspectives*, June 22. http://neweconomicperspectives.org/2012/06/why-latvias-austerity-model-cant-be-exported.html

Hutchinson, Martin. 2011. "The Strong Countries Should Leave the Euro." *Bullion Vault*, September 2. http://goldnews.bullionvault.com/eurozone_breakup_090220115

ILO. 2012a. "Global Employment Trends 2012: Preventing a Deeper Jobs Crisis." *International Labour Organization*. http://www.ilo.org/wcmsp5/groups/public/@dgreports/@dcomm/@publ/documents/publication/wcms_171571.pdf

ILO. 2012b. "Global Wage Report 2012/13." *International Labour Organization*, December 7. http://www.ilo.org/wcmsp5/groups/public/---dgreports/---dcomm/documents/publication/wcms_194844.pdf

IMF. 2013. "Greece: 2013 Article IV Consultation." *International Monetary Fund*, June. http://www.imf.org/external/pubs/ft/scr/2013/cr13154.pdf

IMF Survey Magazine. 2013. "IMF Support for Greece Moves Ahead with €3.24 Billion Disbursement." January 18. http://www.imf.org/external/pubs/ft/survey/so/2013/int011813a.htm

Implementation Body. 2012. "Savings." http://implementationbody.gov.ie/savings/

Islam, Iyanatul, and Anis Chowdhury. 2010. "The Fallacy of Austerity-Based Fiscal Consolidation." *G-24*, Policy Brief No. 58, August 15. http://www.g24.org/Publications/PolicyBriefs/pbno58.pdf

Irish Examiner. 2013. "IMF Admits Underestimating Impact of Austerity in Greece." June 6. http://www.irishexaminer.com/breakingnews/business/imf-admits-underestimating-impact-of-austerity-in-greece-596659.html

James, Steve. 2009. "Ireland: Government to Impose Draconian Austerity Measures with Opposition Support." *World Socialist Web Site*, March 16. https://www.wsws.org/en/articles/2009/03/irel-m16.html

Janssen, Ronald. 2013. "Real Wages in the Eurozone: Not a Double But a Continuing Dip." *Social Europe Journal*, May 27. http://www.social-europe.eu/2013/05/real-wages-in-the-eurozone-not-a-double-but-a-continuing-dip/

Jayadev, Arjun, and Mike Konczal. 2010. "The Boom Not the Slump: The Right Time for Austerity." *University of Massachusetts Boston*, Economics Faculty Publication Series, Paper 26. http://scholarworks.umb.edu/cgi/viewcontent.cgi?article=1026&context=econ_faculty_pubs&sei-redir=1&referer=http%3A%2F%2Fscholar.google.com%2Fscholar%3Fhl%3Den%26q%3Dausterity%2Bgdp%2Bgrowth%26btnG%3D%26as_sdt%3D1%252C39%26as_sdtp%3D#search=%22austerity%20gdp

%20growth%22

Jones, Gavin. 2011. "Italy Austerity Protesters Clash with Police in Rome." *Reuters*, September 14. http://www.reuters.com/article/2011/09/14/italy-austerity-protests-idUSL5E7KE4NC20110914

Jones, Gavin. 2013. "Beppe Grillo and the 5 Star Movement: An In-Depth Look at Italy's New Kingmaker." *Huffington Post*, March 7. http://www.huffingtonpost.com/2013/03/07/beppe-grillo-5-star-movement_n_2826213.html

Jung, Alexander. 2012. "Where Italy Works: An Economic Miracle in the Venetian Hinterlands." *Spiegel International*, August 8. http://www.spiegel.de/international/europe/booming-economy-in-northern-italy-could-be-a-model-for-the-country-a-848759.html

Kambas, Michele. 2011. "Cyprus Parliament Approves Austerity Package." *Reuters*, August 26. http://www.reuters.com/article/2011/08/26/cyprus-austerity-parliament-idUSLDE77P0JQ20110826

Karanikolos, Marina, Philipa Mladovsky, Jonathan Cylus, Sarah Thomson, Sanjay Basu, Savid Stuckler, Johan P. Mackenbach and Martin McKee. 2013. "Financial Crisis, Austerity, and Health in Europe." *Lancet* 381(9874):1323-1331. http://images.derstandard.at/2013/03/27/lancetfinancialcrisiseurope.pdf

Karnite, Raita. 2011. "Austerity Measures Provoke Protests." *European Industrial Relations Observatory*, July 6. http://www.eurofound.europa.eu/eiro/2011/04/articles/LV1104019I.htm

Keep Talking Greece. 2013a. "Stournaras Shocks Greeks: Emergency Property Tax Also in 2013." March 15. http://www.keeptalkinggreece.com/2013/03/15/stournaras-shocks-greeks-emergency-property-tax-also-in-2013/

Keep Talking Greece. 2013b. "Greece Moves Forward: 15,000 Lay-Offs, Minimum Wage at €490/Month, Retroactive Property Levy." April 29. http://www.keeptalkinggreece.com/2013/04/29/greece-moves-forward-15000-lay-offs-minimum-wage-at-e490month-retroactive-property-levy/

Keiller, Agnes Norris, and Larry Elliott. 2011. "George Osborne Told 'Rethink Cuts or Miss Deficit Target'." *Guardian*, August 2. http://www.guardian.co.uk/business/2011/aug/03/george-osborne-miss-deficit-target

Kelland, Kate. 2013. "Spanish Austerity Cuts Put Lives at Risk, Study Finds." *Reuters*, June 13. http://www.reuters.com/article/2013/06/13/us-austerity-spain-idUSBRE95C0DB20130613

Khalip, Andrei. 2010. "Portugal Oks Bills in Austerity Plan, Bonds Dumped."

Reuters, May 7. http://www.reuters.com/article/2010/05/07/businesspro-us-portugal-austerity-idUSTRE6464UY20100507

Khalip, Andrei. 2011. "Update 1- Portugal Scraps Golden Shares in Utilities." *Reuters*, July 5. http://www.reuters.com/article/2011/07/05/portugal-goldenshares-idUSLDE76414L20110705

Khalip, Andrei. 2012. "Lisbon Protests: More than 100,000 Rally against Austerity in Portugal." *Huffington Post*, February 11. http://www.huffingtonpost.com/2012/02/12/portugal-protest-austerity_n_1270438.html

Khalip, Andrei. 2013. "Portuguese March against Austerity, Want Government Out." *Reuters*, March 2. http://www.reuters.com/article/2013/03/02/us-portugal-protests-idUSBRE92109J20130302

Kilkenny, Allison. 2013. "Thousands Protest the UK Government's Brutal Austerity." *Nation*, April 1. http://www.thenation.com/blog/173602/thousands-protest-uk-governments-brutal-austerity#

Kinsella, Stephen. 2011. "Is Ireland Really the Role Model for Austerity?" *University College Dublin*, Working Paper No.22. http://www.ucd.ie/geary/static/publications/workingpapers/gearywp201122.pdf

Kouvoussis, Sypros. 2013. "Crisis Makes Greece 3rd Poorest in EU." *Greek Reporter*, March 27. http://greece.greekreporter.com/2013/03/27/crisis-makes-greece-3d-poorest-in-e-u/

Kowsmann, Patricia. 2011. "Portugal's 2011 Budget Deficit to be Sharply Lower than Target." *Wall Street Journal*, December 13. http://online.wsj.com/article/BT-CO-20111213-704123.html

Krebs, Tom, and Martin Scheffel. 2013. "Macroeconomic Evaluation of Labor Market Reform in Germany." *IMF Economic Review* 61: 664-701.

Krönig, Jürgen. 2013. "Germany in Europe- The Unwilling Hegemon." *Policy Network*, May 7. http://www.policy-network.net/pno_detail.aspx?ID=4393&title=Germany+in+Europe+%E2%80%93+the+unwilling+hegemon+

Kunzmann, Richard. 2012. "The Austerity Britain Report: The Impact of the Recession on the UK's Health, According to GP's." *Insight Research Group*, August. http://www.insightrg.com/downloads/austerity-britain-key-findings-august-2012.pdf

Kuo, Lily. 2013. "Under Austerity, Italians are Scrapping Cars for Bikes." *Quartz*, May 28. http://qz.com/88512/under-austerity-italians-are-scrapping-cars-for-bikes/

Kyero. 2009. "Spain's 2010 Austerity Budget." September 30. http://news.kyero.com/2009/09/30/spain-s-2010-austerity-budget/

Labropoulou, Elinda, and Laura Smith-Spark. 2012. "Greek Parliament Approves Austerity Cuts." *CNN*, November 7. http://www.cnn.com/2012/11/07/world/europe/greece-austerity

Lane, Philip R. 2011. "The Irish Crisis." *World Financial Review*. http://www.worldfinancialreview.com/?p=874

Lapavitsas, Costas, Annina Kaltenbrunner, Duncan Lindo, J. Mitchell, Juan Pablo Painceira, Eugenia Pires, Jeff Powell, Alexis Stenfors and Nuno Teles. 2010. "Eurozone Crisis: Beggar Thyself and Thy Neighbour." *Journal of Balkan and Near Eastern Studies* 12(4):321-373.

Larouchepac. 2013a. "Budget Cuts Taking Down Health Care Systems of Spain and Portugal." May 11. http://larouchepac.com/node/26541

Larouchepac. 2013b. "Cyprus Genocide Through Health Cuts." May 18. http://larouchepac.com/node/26648

Legido-Quigley, Helena, Laura Otero, Daniel la Parra, Carlos Alvarez-Dardet, Jose M. Martin-Moreno and Martin McKee. 2013. "Will Austerity Cuts Dismantle the Spanish Healthcare System?" *British Medical Journal*, No.346. http://www.bmj.com/content/346/bmj.f2363

Lima, Joao. 2013. "Portugal Posts Wider Budget Deficit as Spending Increases." *Businessweek*, June 25. http://www.businessweek.com/news/2013-06-25/portugal-posts-wider-budget-budget-deficit-as-spending-increases

Lindholm, Christer K. 2012. "Does Austerity Work? Lessons from the Latvian Crisis in 2008-2010." In *Baltic Rim Economies Expert Articles 2012*, edited by Leena Koivisto, 99. Electronic Publication of Pan-European Institute, University of Turku. http://www.utu.fi/fi/yksikot/tse/yksikot/PEI/raportit-ja-tietopaketit/Documents/2013/BRE%20Kokoelma%202012_web.pdf

Local. 2013a. "Italy Suicide Wave Shows No Sign of Slowing." June 11. http://www.thelocal.it/20130621/suicide-wave-among-italians-continues

Local. 2013b. "Spain Slashes Spending in Public Sector Overhaul." June 22. http://www.thelocal.es/20130622/spain-to-save-6-5-billion-euro-with-public-sector-overhaul

Lopez, Alejandro. 2013. "Spanish Government Imposes more Austerity Measures." *World Socialist Web Site*, May 30. http://www.wsws.org/en/articles/2013/05/30/spai-m30.html

Loungani, Prakash. 2011. "Will It Hurt? Who Will It Hurt? The Macroeconomic and Distributional Effects of Fiscal Austerity." *International Labour Organization*, UN Expert Group Meeting, Geneva, June 24-25. http://www.ilo.org/wcmsp5/groups/public/@ed_emp/@emp_policy/documents/meetingdocument/wcms_162962.pdf

Mangan, Stephen. 2013. "Irish Marchers Protest Nationwide against Austerity." *Reuters*, February 9.

http://www.reuters.com/article/2013/02/09/us-ireland-debt-idUSBRE9180BH20130209

Marcus, Jon. 2011. "Austerity Measures" Students Protest as a Cash-Strapped Government Lets British Universities Triple Their Fees." In *American Higher Education: Journalistic and Policy Perspectives from National CrossTalk*, edited by William H. Trombley and Todd Sallo (2012), 233-236. San Jose, CA:National Center for Public Policy and Higher Education. http://www.highereducation.org/crosstalk/ctbook/pdfbook/UKAusterityMeasuresBookLayout.pdf . (For full volume access http://www.highereducation.org/crosstalk/ctbook/pdfbook/CrossTalkBook.pdf.)

Margeirsson, Olafur. 2013. "New Info on the Amount of Household Debt canceled in Iceland." *News of Iceland*, June 24. http://www.newsoficeland.com/home/icelandic-economics/item/1779-new-info-on-the-amount-of-household-debt-canceled-in-iceland

Marx, Karl. 1850. "The Class Struggles in France, 1848 to 1850." *Neue Rheinische Zeitung Revue.* http://www.marxists.org/archive/marx/works/1850/class-struggles-france/ch01.htm

McDonald, Henry. 2012. "Ireland Budget Imposes more Austerity." *Guardian*, December 5. http://www.guardian.co.uk/world/2012/dec/05/ireland-austerity-budget

McDonald, Henry. 2013. "Ireland Falls Back into Recession Despite Multibillion-Euro Austerity Drive." *Guardian*, June 27. http://www.guardian.co.uk/business/2013/jun/27/ireland-back-recession-austerity-data-revision

McKee, Martin, Marina Karanikolos, Paul Belcher, and David Stuckler. 2012. "Austerity: A Failed Experiment on the People of Europe." *Clinical Medicine* 12(4):346-350. http://www.clinmed.rcpjournal.org/content/12/4/346.short; http://ideas.repec.org/p/lev/levypn/12-11.html

McKittrick, David. 2012. "Ireland's Austerity D-Day: How Much Pain Can it Take?" *Independent*, May 30. http://www.independent.co.uk/news/world/europe/irelands-austerity-dday-how-much-pain-can-it-take-7800898.html

Menendez, Lia. 2012. "The Spread of the European Sovereign Debt Crisis." *University of Iowa*, Center for International Finance and Development. http://ebook.law.uiowa.edu/ebook/uicifd-ebook/part-6-ii-spread-european-sovereign-debt-crisis

Mignone, Mario B. 2008. *Italy Today: Facing the Challenges of the New Millenium.* New York: Peter Lang.

Ministry of Economy and Competitiveness. 2012. "Labour Market Reform." *Government of Spain*, February.

http://www.thespanisheconomy.com/SiteCollectionDocuments/en-gb/Economic%20Policy%20Measures/120517%20labour%20market%20reform,%20brief%20description.pdf

Mitchell, Paul. 2012. "Thousands Demonstrate against New Budget in Portugal." *World Socialist Web Site*, October 18. http://www.wsws.org/en/articles/2012/10/port-o18.html

Mitchell, Susan. 2012. "Hospital Waiting Times up by 24% under Coalition." *Sunday Business Post*, 20 May.

Mladovsky, Philipa, Divya Srivastava, Jonathan Cylus, Marina Karanikolos, Tamas Evetovits, Sarah Thomson, and Martin McKee. 2012. "Health Policy Responses to the Financial Crisis in Europe." *World Health Organization,* Policy Summary 5. http://www.euro.who.int/__data/assets/pdf_file/0009/170865/e96643.pdf

Moffett, Matt, and Art Patnaude. 2013. "Spain Rethinks Austerity." *Wall Street Journal*, April 26. http://online.wsj.com/article/SB10001424127887324474004578446573412012466.html

Monson, Guy, and Subitha Subramaniam. 2010. "Austerity Drives Can Unleash Confidence". *Financial Times*, July 27.

Moral-Arce, Ignacio. 2013. "Aplicacion de Factores de Sostenibilidad en el Sistema de Pensiones Espanol: Previsiones Para el Periodo 2012-2050." *Instituto de Estudios Fiscales*, No.4. http://www.ief.es/documentos/recursos/publicaciones/papeles_trabajo/2013_04.pdf

Morris, Nigel. 2010. "One by One, the Quangos Are Abolished. But at What Cost?" *Independent*, July 27. http://www.independent.co.uk/news/uk/politics/one-by-one-the-quangos-are-abolished-but-at-what-cost-2036175.html

Morris, Nigel. 2013. "Benefit Cuts Sends Number of Food Bank Users Soaring." *Independent*, July 11. http://www.independent.co.uk/news/uk/politics/benefit-cuts-sends-number-of-food-bank-users-soaring-8701367.html

Morrison, Sarah. 2012. "Austerity Brings out Protesters." *Independent*, October 21. http://www.independent.co.uk/news/uk/politics/austerity-brings-out-the-protesters-8219528.html

Moss, Vincent, and Ben Glaze. 2013. "Austerity Britain: Crippling Benefit Cuts Will Leave Families £891 Worse off this Year." *Mirror*, March 31. http://www.mirror.co.uk/news/uk-news/austerity-britain-crippling-benefit-cuts-1793727

Mulas-Granados, Carlos. 2005. "Fiscal Adjustments and the Short-term Trade-Off between Economic Growth and Equality." *Hacienda Pública Española / Revista de Economía Pública* 172(1):61-92. http://www.ief.es/documentos/recursos/publicaciones/revistas/hac_pu

b/172_Mulas.pdf
Nadeau, Barbie Latza. 2012. "Europe's Austerity Crisis Ravages Italy's South." *Daily Beast*, October 2. http://www.thedailybeast.com/articles/2012/10/02/europe-s-austerity-crisis-ravages-italy-s-south.html

NBC News. 2012. "Ireland Austerity: Hospitals to Send Some Patients Home on Weekends." August 31, http://worldnews.nbcnews.com/_news/2012/08/31/13586353-ireland-austerity-hospitals-to-send-some-patients-home-on-weekends?lite

New York Times. 2010. "Italy: Austerity Package Wins Vote of Confidence." July 28. http://www.nytimes.com/2010/07/29/world/europe/29briefs-Italy.html

O'Brien, Dan. 2013. "Ireland Faces Two More Years of Austerity." *Irish Times*, April 30. http://www.irishtimes.com/business/economy/ireland/ireland-faces-two-more-years-of-austerity-1.1378222

O'Brien, Dan, and Ciara Kenny. 2013. "Rise in Numbers Working Part-Time Sees Unemployment Fall to 13.7%." *Irish Times*, May 30. http://www.irishtimes.com/business/economy/ireland/rise-in-numbers-working-part-time-sees-unemployment-fall-to-13-7-1.1411534

OCCRP. 2011. "Latvian Bank Woes." *Organized Crime and Corruption Reporting Project*, October 30. http://www.reportingproject.net/proxy/en/latvian-bank-woes

O'Connell, Hugh. 2013. "The Croke Park Agreement Saved Taxpayer €1.8 Billion." *Journal*, July 3. http://www.thejournal.ie/croke-park-savings-977403-Jul2013/

O'Connor, Nat. 2011. "Ireland's Austerity Woes." *Social Europe Journal*, February 7. http://www.social-europe.eu/2011/02/irelands-austerity-woes/

O'Grady, Peadar. 2012. "Economic Crisis: Austerity and Privatisation in Health-Care in Ireland." *Irish Marxist Review* 1(2):13-23. http://www.irishmarxistreview.net/index.php/imr/article/view/25/28

OECD. 2010. "OECD Economic Surveys: Germany 2010." *Organization for Economic Development and Co-operation*, March.

OECD. 2011. "OECD Economic Surveys: Greece 2011." *Organization for Economic Development and Co-operation*, August.

Onaran, Özlem, and Giorgos Galanis. 2012. "Is Aggregate Demand Wage-led or Profit-led? National and Global Effects." *International Labour Organization*, Conditions of Work and Employment Series, No. 40. http://www.ilo.org/wcmsp5/groups/public/---ed_protect/---protrav/---travail/documents/publication/wcms_192121.pdf

O'Regan, Michael. 2013. "Quinn Defends Education Cuts." *Irish Times*, January 16. http://www.irishtimes.com/news/quinn-defends-

education-cuts-1.1071300
Owen, Paul. 2013. "Budget 2013- the Key Points." *Guardian*, March 20. http://www.guardian.co.uk/uk/2013/mar/20/budget-2013-key-points-live?INTCMP=SRCH
Parkin, Brian. 2013. "Cyprus to Sell Gold to Help Overcome 'Challenging' Debt Outlook." *Bloomberg*, April 10. http://www.bloomberg.com/news/2013-04-10/cyprus-to-sell-gold-to-help-overcome-challenging-debt-outlook.html
Parkinson, Joe. 2011. "Cyprus Tries to Avoid Greek Contagion." *Wall Street Journal*, July 25. http://online.wsj.com/article/SB10001424053111190359110457646615 0495822720.html
Paterson, Tony. 2013. "Latvia's Reward for Austerity? Membership of the Euro in 2014." *Independent*, June 5. http://www.independent.co.uk/news/world/europe/latvias-reward-for-austerity-membership-of-the-euro-in-2014-8646364.html
Pereira, Alvaro Santos, and Pedro Lains. 2012. "From an Agrarian Society to a Knowledge Economy? The Rising Importance of Education to the Portuguese Economy, 1950-2009." In *Higher Education in Portugal 1974-2009: A Nation, A Generation*, edited by Guy R. Neave and Alberto Amaral. Dordrecht: Springer.
Perotti, Roberto. 2011. "The 'Austerity Myth': Gain without Pain?" *National Bureau of Economic Research*, Working Papers, No. 17571. http://www.nber.org/papers/w17571
Persson, Mats. 2013. "Is Cyprus Turning into a Zombie Economy?" *Telegraph*, April 4. http://blogs.telegraph.co.uk/finance/matspersson/100023894/is-cyprus-turning-into-a-zombie-economy/
Petras, James. 2013. "Austerity, Mass Unemployment and Emigration in the European Union: Ireland and the Basque Country." *Global Research*, May 30. http://www.globalresearch.ca/austerity-mass-unemployment-and-emigration-in-the-european-union-ireland-and-the-basque-country/5336922
Pettinger, Tejvan. 2012. "Spanish Economic Crisis Summary." *Economics Help*, July 13. http://www.economicshelp.org/blog/5525/economics/spanish-economic-crisis-summary/
Pietras, Jennifer. 2009. "Austerity Measures in the EU- A Country by Country Table." *European Institute*. http://www.europeaninstitute.org/Special-G-20-Issue-on-Financial-Reform/austerity-measures-in-the-eu.html
Pisa, Nick, and Oliver Pickup. 2011. "Italy Grinds to a Halt as Three Million Stike over €45bn Austerity Package." *Daily Mail,* September 7. http://www.dailymail.co.uk/news/article-2034352/Italy-strike-THREE-million-protest-austerity-package.html

Press TV. 2013a. "Spain's Medical Workers Strike over Hospital Privatization." May 8. http://www.presstv.com/detail/2013/05/08/302408/spanish-health-workers-hold-strike/

Press TV. 2013b. "Portuguese Protesters Urge Government to Quit over Austerity Bid." July 12. http://www.presstv.ir/detail/2013/07/12/313417/portuguese-activists-urge-govt-to-quit/

Prosser, Thomas. 2011. "United Kingdom: EIRO Annual Review 2009." *European Industrial Relations Observatory*, January 11. http://www.eurofound.europa.eu/eiro/studies/tn1004019s/uk1004019q.htm

Psyllides, George. 2013. "Stung Depositors Will Not Foot Bank Lay-Off Bill, Union Pledges." *Cyprus Mail*, July 1. http://cyprus-mail.com/2013/07/01/stung-depositors-will-not-foot-bank-lay-off-bill-union-pledges/

Ragioneria Generale dello Stato. 2010."Conto Annuale" *Ministero dell' Economia e delle Finanze*. Available from: http://www.rgs.mef.gov.it/VERSIONE-I/RGS-comuni/Note-per-l/2011/Pubblicato1/.

Rapoza, Kenneth. 2012. "Euro Down: Worst Case Scenarios Becoming More Plausible." *Forbes*, May 30. http://www.forbes.com/sites/kenrapoza/2012/05/30/imagining-a-eurozone-break-down/

Rastrigina, Olga, and Anna Zasova. 2012. "The Distributional Impact of Austerity Measures in Latvia." *Forum for Research on Eastern European and Emerging Economies*, February 6. http://freepolicybriefs.org/2012/02/06/the-distributional-impact-of-austerity-measures-in-latvia/

Reilly, Gavan. 2012. "Average Industrial Wage Down by 3.2 Per Cent in Second Quarter." *Journal*, August 29. http://businessetc.thejournal.ie/average-industrial-wage-in-ireland-576846-Aug2012/

Reinhart, Carmen M., and Kenneth S. Rogoff. 2010. "Growth in a Time of Debt." *American Economic Review* 100(2):573-578.

Reinhart, Carmen M., and Kenneth S. Rogoff. 2013. "Reinhart and Rogoff: Responding to Our Critics." *New York Times*, April 25. http://www.nytimes.com/2013/04/26/opinion/reinhart-and-rogoff-responding-to-our-critics.html?pagewanted=all

Reuters. 2012. "Spending Cuts Best Path to Faster Growth.-Gaspar." April 18. http://www.reuters.com/article/2012/04/18/economy-portugal-gaspar-idUSL2E8FINTY20120418

Revolting Europe. 2012. "Italians Pay out Billions to Fight Sickness as Public Health System Cuts Bite." March 17. http://revolting-europe.com/2012/03/17/italian-pay-out-billions-to-fight-sickness-as-

public-health-system-cuts-bite/
Rial, Nerea. 2011. "Parliament Gives Final Green Light to Austerity Budget." *New Europe*, December 4. http://www.neurope.eu/article/parliament-gives-final-green-light-austerity-budget
Riley, Charles. 2013. "Even Abenomics Can't Ignore Japan Debt." *CNN Money*, April 23.
http://money.cnn.com/2013/04/23/news/economy/japan-debt-abenomics/index.html
Rodrik, Dani. 1996. "Understanding Economic Policy Reform." *Journal of Economic Literature* 34(1):9-41.
http://www.vedegylet.hu/fejkrit/szvggyujt/Rodrik_UnderstandingEconomicPolicyReforms.pdf
Roman, David, and Ilan Brat. 2013. "Spain's Central Bank Seeks Minimum Wage Suspension." *Wall Street Journal*, May 31.
http://online.wsj.com/article/SB10001424127887324682204578517240528279954.html
Rosales, Arturo. 2012. "Privatizing Healthcare in Spain. Making People Pay for Financial Mis-Management." *Axis of Logic*, December 27.
http://axisoflogic.com/artman/publish/Article_65253.shtml
RT. 2012. "One in Five UK Workers Earns Below a Living Wage- Research." *Russia Today*, October 30. http://rt.com/business/uk-workers-living-wage-research-552/
RT. 2013. "Worst Cuts in Wages for UK Workers in 'Deepest Recession Since WWII', IFS Shows." *Russia Today*, June 12.
http://rt.com/news/workers-cut-wages-recession-570/
RTE News. 2009. "Public Service Pension Levy Announced." *Raidió Teilifís Éireann*, February 3. http://www.rte.ie/news/2009/0203/113483-economy/
RTE News. 2011a. "Portugal Toughens Austerity in 2012 Budget." *Raidió Teilifís Éireann*, October 14.
http://www.rte.ie/news/business/2011/1014/307445-portugal/
RTE News. 2011b. "Spain Faces €15 Billion of Austerity Measures." *Raidió Teilifís Éireann*, December 30.
http://www.rte.ie/news/business/2011/1230/310392-spain/
RTE News. 2012. "Ireland Passes Fiscal Treaty Referendum by 60.3% to 39.7%." *Raidió Teilifís Éireann*, July 26.
http://www.rte.ie/news/2012/0601/323199-fiscal-treaty-referendum-count-to-begin/
RWER Blog. 2013. "Some Recent Data on the EU." *Real World Economics Review Blog*, July 5. http://rwer.wordpress.com/2013/07/05/some-recent-data-on-the-eu/
Ryan, Susan. 2012. "14.5 Per Cent of Dwellings in Ireland Vacant in Census 2011." *Journal*, March 29. http://www.thejournal.ie/14-5-per-cent-of-dwellings-in-ireland-vacant-in-census-2011-400231-Mar2012/

Sansone, Kurt. 2013. "Understanding the Cypriot Bank Crisis." *Times of Malta*, March 31. http://www.timesofmalta.com/articles/view/20130331/local/Understanding-the-Cypriot-bank-crisis.463528

Schifrin, Nick. 2012. "Ferrari Crackdown: Italy Declaring War on Tax Cheats." *ABC News*, May 22. http://abcnews.go.com/International/ferrari-crackdown-italy-declaring-war-tax-cheats/story?id=16401014#.UdIW8fnqnMo

Schultz, Stefan. 2012. "Not the Next Greece: Portugal Can Still Turn the Corner in Debt Crisis." *Spiegel International*, March 23. http://www.spiegel.de/international/europe/what-portugal-needs-to-do-to-get-out-of-the-crisis-a-823318.html

Shah, Neil. 2010. "Ireland Outlines Austerity Measures." *Wall Street Journal*, November 25. http://online.wsj.com/article/SB10001424052748703572404575634452116491286.html

Shilton, Jordan. 2013. "Irish Government and Trade Unions Deepen Austerity Measures." *World Socialist Web Site*, March 4. http://www.wsws.org/en/articles/2013/03/04/irel-m04.html

Simonazzi, Annamaria, Andrea Ginzburg, and Gianluigi Nocella. 2013. "Economic Relations Between Germany and Southern Europe." *Cambridge Journal of Economics* 37(3):653-675. http://cje.oxfordjournals.org/content/37/3/653.full

Sivy, Michael. 2012. "Why Germany Should Leave the Euro Zone." *Time*, April 12. http://business.time.com/2012/04/12/why-germany-should-leave-the-eurozone/

Skidelsky, Robert. 2013. "Economic Rebalancing Acts." *Project Syndicate*, June 30. http://www.project-syndicate.org/commentary/the-incompatibility-of-austerity-and-economic-reform-by-robert-skidelsky

Sky News. 2012. "Ireland Budget: More Austerity Measures." December 5. http://news.sky.com/story/1021182/ireland-budget-more-austerity-measures

Sommers, Jeffrey, and Michael Hudson. 2013. "Latvia's Economic Disaster Heralded as a Neoliberal 'Success Story': A Model for Europe and the US?" *Global Research*, January 3. http://www.globalresearch.ca/latvias-economic-disaster-heralded-as-a-neoliberal-success-story-a-model-for-europe-and-the-us/5317675

Sovereign. 2011. "Cyprus MPs Approve Austerity Measures Package." August 31. http://www.sovereigngroup.com/offshore-news/sovereign-news/1235/0/Cyprus+MPs+approve+austerity+measures+package.html

Speciale, Alessandro. 2011. "Italy: Austerity, Berlusconi-style." *Global Post*, October 36.

  http://www.globalpost.com/dispatch/news/regions/europe/italy/111026/austerity-berlusconi-italy-EU-summit
Spiegel. 2010. "Striking against Austerity: Unions Shut Down Portugal over Planned Cuts." November 24.
  http://www.spiegel.de/international/europe/striking-against-austerity-unions-shut-down-portugal-over-planned-cuts-a-730905.html
Squires, Nick. 2010. "Advance Guard of Angry Women Lead Italians into European Protests over Austerity Cuts." *Telegraph*, May 29.
  http://www.telegraph.co.uk/news/worldnews/europe/italy/7783603/Advance-guard-of-angry-women-lead-Italians-into-European-protests-over-austerity-cuts.html
Squires, Nick. 2012. "Italian Businessman Becomes Country's 25th 'Austerity Suicide' of the Year." *Telegraph*, April 30.
  http://www.telegraph.co.uk/news/worldnews/europe/italy/9236231/Italian-businessman-becomes-countrys-25th-austerity-suicide-of-the-year.html
Stavrakis, Charilaos. 2009. "The Cyprus Economy and Its Economic Role in Europe." *World Commerce Review* 3(3):1-2.
  http://www.worldcommercereview.com/publications/article_pdf/135
Steinberg, Stefan. 2011a. "Resignation of Italy's Berlusconi Clears Way for 'Technocratic' Government Chosen by the Banks." *World Socialist Web Site*, November 14. http://www.wsws.org/en/articles/2011/11/italn14.html
Steinberg, Stefan. 2011b. "Italy: Technocrat Monti Introduces New Drastic Austerity Package." *World Socialist Web Site*, December 6.
  http://www.wsws.org/en/articles/2011/12/ital-d06.html
Stevens, Robert. 2013. "European Union Imposes Austerity Bailout on Cyprus." *World Socialist Web Site,* April 9.
  http://www.wsws.org/en/articles/2013/04/09/cypr-a09.html
Stiglitz, Joseph E. 2012. *The Price of Inequality: How Today's Divided Society Endangers Our Future.* New York: W.W. Norton & Company.
Stock Market Watch. 2013. "Italy Announced a New Economic Stimulus Plan is Called 'a Revolution'." June 17.
  http://www.thestockmarketwatch.co/italy-announced-a-new-economic-stimulus-plan-is-called-a-revolution.html
Stuckler, David, and Sanjay Basu. 2013a. "How Austerity Kills." *New York Times*, May 12. http://www.nytimes.com/2013/05/13/opinion/how-austerity-kills.html?pagewanted=all&_r=0
Stuckler, David, and Sanjay Basu. 2013b. *The Body Economic: Why Austerity Kills.* New York: Basic Books.
Suoninen, Sakari, and Marc Jones. 2013. "Factbox- How ECB's Emergency Liquidity Assistance Works." *Reuters*, March 21.
  http://uk.reuters.com/article/2013/03/21/uk-factbox-ecbs-emergency-idUKBRE92K0DT20130321

Tagaris, Karolina, and Michele Kambas. 2013. "Cyprus Weighs Big Bank Levy; Bailout Goes Down to Wire." *Reuters,* March 23. http://www.reuters.com/article/2013/03/23/us-cyprus-parliament-idUSBRE92G03I20130323

Taipei Times. 2011. "Thousands Rally against Austerity Plans in Portugal." October 3. http://www.taipeitimes.com/News/biz/archives/2011/10/03/2003514776

Tanner, Michael D. 2012. "Austerity Works." *Cato Institute,* June 20. http://www.cato.org/publications/commentary/austerity-works?print

Telegraph. 2009. "Ireland Raises Taxes in Austerity Budget and Unveils Agency to Buy Toxic Assets." April 7. http://www.telegraph.co.uk/finance/5121018/Ireland-raises-taxes-in-austerity-budget-and-unveils-agency-to-buy-toxic-assets.html

Telegraph. 2013. "Homeless People being Forced to Live in Caves." June 12. http://www.telegraph.co.uk/news/politics/10115005/Homeless-people-being-forced-to-live-in-caves.html

Theodoropoulou, Sotiria and Andre Watt 2011. "Withdrawal Symptoms: An Assessment of the Austerity Packages in Europe" *European Trade Union Institute,* Working Paper. http://www.etui.org/Publications2/Working-Papers/Withdrawal-symptoms-an-assessment-of-the-austerity-packages-in-Europe

Thompson, Mark. 2013. "IMF Cuts Global Growth Forecast." *CNN Money,* April 16. http://money.cnn.com/2013/04/16/news/economy/economy-imf/index.html

Thomson, Ainsley. 2013. "U.K. Plans for More Austerity in 2015." *Wall Street Journal,* June 26. http://online.wsj.com/article/SB10001424127887323419604578569330360660240.html

Totaro, Paola. 2008. "UK Unveils $47b Stimulus Plan." *Sydney Morning Herald,* November 25. http://www.smh.com.au/business/world-business/uk-unveils-47b-stimulus-plan-20081125-6g9c.html

Tremlett, Giles. 2012. "Portuguese Death Rate Rise Linked to Pain of Austerity Programme." *Guardian,* March 19. http://www.guardian.co.uk/business/2012/mar/19/portuguese-death-rate-rise-austerity-programme

Tremlett, Giles. 2013a. "Portugal's Unemployment Rate Hits 18%." *Guardian,* May 9. http://www.guardian.co.uk/world/2013/may/09/portugal-unemployment-government-cuts

Tremlett, Giles. 2013b. "Spanish Wages Depressed amid Eurozone Crisis." *Guardian,* May 31. http://www.guardian.co.uk/world/2013/may/31/spanish-wages-depressed-eurozone-crisis

Trotman, Andrew. 2013. "Ikea Founder Ingvar Kamprad Moves Back to

Sweden after 40 Years in Switzerland." *Telegraph*, June 26. http://www.telegraph.co.uk/finance/newsbysector/retailandconsumer/10145042/Ikea-founder-Ingvar-Kamprad-moves-back-to-Sweden-after-40-years-in-Switzerland.html

Ummelas, Ott. 2013. "Cyprus Woes to Help Latvia Lure Russian Cash, Trigon Says." *Bloomberg*, March 21. http://www.bloomberg.com/news/2013-03-21/cyprus-woes-to-help-latvia-lure-russian-cash-trigon-says.html

Verger, Antoni. 2013. "Austerity and Education Reforms in Spain: Moving Far from International Excellence." *Education in Crisis*, May 8. http://educationincrisis.net/blog/item/894-austerity-and-education-reforms-in-spain-moving-far-away-from-international-excellence

Vina, Gonzalo, Robert Hutton, and Thomas Penny. 2013. "Osborne Pledges Five More Years of U.K. Austerity." *Bloomberg*, March 21. http://www.bloomberg.com/news/2013-03-20/osborne-pledges-five-more-years-of-u-k-austerity.html

Warner, Jeremy. 2012. "Roll up for Britain's £750Bn Corporate Cash Mountain." *Telegraph*, March 28. http://www.telegraph.co.uk/finance/comment/jeremywarner/9172381/Roll-up-for-Britains-750bn-corporate-cash-mountain.html

Warner, Jeremy. 2013. "The Killing of Britain's Economic Salvation: An Export-led Recovery." *Telegraph*, April 26. http://blogs.telegraph.co.uk/finance/jeremywarner/100024274/the-killing-of-britains-economic-salvation-an-export-led-recovery/

Wearden, Graeme. 2013. "Cypriots Protest as UK Strives for Laiki Deal- as It Happened." *Guardian*, March 26. http://www.guardian.co.uk/business/2013/mar/26/eurozone-crisis-cyprus-banks

Weisbrot, Mark and Rebecca Ray. 2009. "Latvia's Internal Devaluation: A Success Story?" *Center for Economic and Policy Research*. http://www.cepr.net/documents/publications/latvia-2011-12.pdf

Werdigier, Julia. 2011. "Its Growth Slowing, Britain Extends Austerity Measures." *New York Times*, November 29. http://www.nytimes.com/2011/11/30/business/global/britain-lowers-economic-growth-forecast.html?_r=0

Wharton. 2013. "Reforming the European Welfare State." *Knowledge @ Wharton*, March 6. http://www.wharton.universia.net/index.cfm?fa=viewArticle&id=2325&language=english

White, Rossa. 2009. "Irish Banking Liabilities." *Davy Research*, February 17. http://www.davy.ie/content/pubarticles/econcr20090217.pdf

Wilkinson, Richard, and Kate Pickett. 2010. *The Spirit Level: Why Equality is Better for Everyone.* London: Penguin.

Winnett, Robert and Andrew Porter. 2008. "Financial Crisis: £500 Billion Bail-Out Plan Helps Stabilise Banks." *Telegraph*, October 9.

> http://www.telegraph.co.uk/finance/financialcrisis/3162206/Financial-crisis-500-billion-bail-out-plan-helps-stabilise-banks.html

Wintour, Patrick and Larry Elliott. 2012. "Budget 2012: Pensioners Fund Tax Cut." *Guardian*, March 21.
> http://www.guardian.co.uk/uk/2012/mar/21/budget-2012-pensioners-tax-cut

Wolf, Martin. 2010. "A Question for Chancellor Osborne" *Financial Times*, June 10.

Wolf, Martin. 2012. "The Impact of Fiscal Austerity in the Eurozone." *Financial Times*, April 27. http://blogs.ft.com/martin-wolf-exchange/2012/04/27/the-impact-of-fiscal-austerity-in-the-eurozone/?Authorised=false#axzz1uBslfOlo

Woolfe, Zachary. 2013. "Now Onstage in Spain: Austerity." *New York Times*, February 15. http://www.nytimes.com/2013/02/17/arts/music/in-spain-austerity-takes-to-the-stage.html?pagewanted=all&_r=0

World Service Conference of Narcotics Anonymous. 1981.
> http://www.amonymifoundation.org/uploads/NA_Approval_Form_Scan.pdf

Yglesias, Matthew. 2013. "Latvia's Sad Strange 'Success'." *Slate*, January 2.
> http://www.slate.com/blogs/moneybox/2013/01/02/latvian_austerity_a_terrifying_success_story.html

Young, Brigitte, and Willi Semmler. 2011. "The European Sovereign Debt Crisis: Is Germany to Blame?" *German Politics and Society* 97(20): 1-24.

Zitko, Mislav. 2012. "The Social Consequences of Imposed Austerity: The Case of Education." *Green European Journal* 2:17-22.
> http://www.greeneuropeanjournal.eu/wp-content/uploads/2012/05/GEF-Journal-art-3.pdf

Figures

Illustration 1: "Austerity Measures and Impact on GDP."
Morrison, Michael. 2012. "Evidence Suggest Austerity Programs Fail in Economic Downturns." Decisions on Evidence, May 8.
> http://www.decisionsonevidence.com/2012/05/evidence-suggests-austerity-programs-fail-in-economic-downturns/

Illustration 2: "Spain Government Budget Balance."
Trading Economics, "Spain Government Budget."
> http://www.tradingeconomics.com/spain/government-budget

Illustration 3: "Spain Government Debt-to-GDP Ratio."
Trading Economics, "Spain Government Debt to GDP."
> http://www.tradingeconomics.com/spain/government-debt-to-gdp

Illustration 4: "Spain Annual GDP Growth Rate."
Trading Economics, "Spain GDP Annual Growth Rate."
    http://www.tradingeconomics.com/spain/gdp-growth-annual

Illustration 5: "Spain Unemployment Rate."
Trading Economics, "Spain Unemployment Rate."
    http://www.tradingeconomics.com/spain/unemployment-rate

Illustration 6: "Portugal Government Budget Balance."
Trading Economics, "Portugal Government Budget."
    http://www.tradingeconomics.com/portugal/government-budget

Illustration 7: "Portugal Government Debt-to-GDP Ratio."
Trading Economics, "Portugal Government Debt to GDP."
    http://www.tradingeconomics.com/portugal/government-debt-to-gdp

Illustration 8: "Portugal Annual GDP Growth Rate."
Trading Economics, "Portugal GDP Annual Growth Rate."
    http://www.tradingeconomics.com/portugal/gdp-growth-annual

Illustration 9: "Portugal Unemployment Rate."
Trading Economics, "Portugal Unemployment Rate."
    http://www.tradingeconomics.com/portugal/unemployment-rate

Illustration 10: "Italy Government Budget Balance."
Trading Economics, "Italy Government Budget."
    http://www.tradingeconomics.com/italy/government-budget

Illustration 11: "Italy Government Debt-to-GDP Ratio."
Trading Economics, "Italy Government Debt to GDP."
    http://www.tradingeconomics.com/italy/government-debt-to-gdp

Illustration 12: "Italy Annual GDP Growth Rate."
Trading Economics, "Italy GDP Annual Growth Rate."
    http://www.tradingeconomics.com/italy/gdp-growth-annual

Illustration 13: "Italy Unemployment Rate."
Trading Economics, "Italy Unemployment Rate."
    http://www.tradingeconomics.com/italy/unemployment-rate

Illustration 14: "Cyprus Annual GDP Growth Rate."
Trading Economics, "Cyprus GDP Annual Growth Rate."
    http://www.tradingeconomics.com/cyprus/gdp-growth-annual

Illustration 15: "Cyprus Government Budget Balance."
Trading Economics, "Cyprus Government Budget."
   http://www.tradingeconomics.com/cyprus/government-budget

Illustration 16: "Cyprus Government Debt-to-GDP Ratio."
Trading Economics, "Cyprus Government Debt to GDP."
   http://www.tradingeconomics.com/cyprus/government-debt-to-gdp

Illustration 17: "Cyprus Unemployment Rate."
Trading Economics, "Cyprus Unemployment Rate."
   http://www.tradingeconomics.com/cyprus/unemployment-rate

Illustration 18: "Ireland Government Budget Balance."
Trading Economics, "Ireland Government Budget."
   http://www.tradingeconomics.com/ireland/government-budget

Illustration 19: "Ireland Government Debt-to-GDP Ratio."
Trading Economics, "Ireland Government Debt to GDP."
   http://www.tradingeconomics.com/ireland/government-debt-to-gdp

Illustration 20: "Ireland Annual GDP Growth Rate."
Trading Economics, "Ireland GDP Annual Growth Rate."
   http://www.tradingeconomics.com/ireland/gdp-growth-annual

Illustration 21: "Ireland Unemployment Rate."
Trading Economics, "Ireland Unemployment Rate."
   http://www.tradingeconomics.com/ireland/unemployment-rate

Illustration 22: "United Kingdom Government Budget Balance."
Trading Economics, "United Kingdom Government Budget."
   http://www.tradingeconomics.com/united-kingdom/government-budget

Illustration 23: "United Kingdom Government Debt-to-GDP Ratio."
Trading Economics, "United Kingdom Government Debt to GDP."
   http://www.tradingeconomics.com/united-kingdom/government-debt-to-gdp

Illustration 24: "United Kingdom Annual GDP Growth Rate."
Trading Economics, "United Kingdom GDP Annual Growth Rate."
   http://www.tradingeconomics.com/united-kingdom/gdp-growth-annual

Illustration 25: "United Kingdom Unemployment Rate."
Trading Economics, "United Kingdom Unemployment Rate."
http://www.tradingeconomics.com/united-kingdom/unemployment-rate

Illustration 26: "United Kingdom Government Budget Balance."
Trading Economics, "United Kingdom Government Budget."
http://www.tradingeconomics.com/latvia/government-budget

Illustration 27: "Latvia Government Debt-to-GDP Ratio."
Trading Economics, "Latvia Government Debt to GDP."
http://www.tradingeconomics.com/latvia/government-debt-to-gdp

Illustration 28: "Latvia Unemployment Rate."
Trading Economics, "Latvia Unemployment Rate."
http://www.tradingeconomics.com/latvia/unemployment-rate

Illustration 29: "Latvia Annual GDP Growth Rate."
Trading Economics, "Latvia GDP Annual Growth Rate."
http://www.tradingeconomics.com/latvia/gdp-growth-annual

Illustration 30: "Latvia's Real GDP in Comparison with the U.S., U.K. and Iceland"
O'Brien, Matthew. 2013. "Sorry, Latvia is No Austerity Success Story." Atlantic, January 3.
http://www.theatlantic.com/business/archive/2013/01/sorry-latvia-is-no-austerity-success-story/266774/

Illustration 31: "Greece: Contributions to GDP"
IMF. 2013. "Greece: 2013 Article IV Consultation." International Monetary Fund, June. http://www.imf.org/external/pubs/ft/scr/2013/cr13154.pdf (p.7)

Illustration 32: "Interest Rates on 10-Year Government Bonds in Various Eurozone Countries"
Micossi, Stefano. 2012. "Bring the Eurozone Back from the Precipice: AN Agenda for the European Council." *VoxEu*, June 21.
http://www.voxeu.org/article/bringing-eurozone-back-precipice-proposal

Illustration 33: "Exchange Rate of Euro against the Dollar for Different Euro Countries"
Fidler, Stephen. 2013. "Euro's Recovery Not Wthout Pain for Some." Wall Street Journal, February 7.

http://online.wsj.com/article/SB10001424127887324590904578290110164764612.html

Illustration 34: "Current Account Balance in Different Eurozone Countries"
Hamodia. 2013. "ECB Cuts Benchmark Interest Rate to 0.5 Percent." May 3.
http://hamodia.com/2013/05/03/ecb-cuts-benchmark-interest-rate-to-0-5-percent/

Illustration 35: "Interest Rate of the Central Banks"
http://macroexposure.com/2011/12/10/current-account-imbalances-in-the-eurozone/

Illustration 36: "Total Bailout Funds for Peripheral EU Countries"
Herbert, Gerhardt, Brian L. Kloss, and Regina G. Borromeo. 2012. "Global High Yield Perspectives." Brandywine Global Investment Management LLC, March 31.
http://www.zerohedge.com/sites/default/files/images/user5/imageroot/2012/05-2/Brandywine%20Global%20Q1%202012.pdf

Illustration 37: "Comparison of Unit Labor Costs"
Economist. 2013. "The Merkel Plan." June 15.
http://www.economist.com/news/special-report/21579144-germanys-vision-europe-all-about-making-continent-more-competitive-merkel

Illustration 38: "Fiscal Transfers in the U.S."
Thompson, Derek. 2012. "The Difference Between the U.S. And Europe in 1 Graph." Atlantic, May 8.
http://www.theatlantic.com/business/archive/2012/05/the-difference-between-the-us-and-europe-in-1-graph/256857/

Illustration 39: "European Regional Development Fund 2007-13"
Wikipedia. 2013. "European Regional Development Fund." February 25.
http://en.wikipedia.org/wiki/European_Regional_Development_Fund

Appendix A

I have listed the countries' budget balance, debt-to-GDP ratio, GDP growth and unemployment rate between 2007-13. All of these European countries have embarked on austerity at least since 2010. The source for all data is the website Trading Economics (http://www.tradingeconomics.com/).

Country-by-Country Table

Greece	Budget balance (% of GDP)	Debt-to-GDP ratio (%)	Annual GDP growth (%)	Unemployment rate (%)
2007	-6.5	105.4	6.2	8.7
2008	-9.8	112.9	0.1	7.9
2009	-15.6	129.7	-4.2	9
2010	-10.7	148.3	-1	11.5
2011	-9.5	170.3	-8.8	15.8
2012	-10	156.9	-6.7	22.3
2013	N/A	N/A	-5.6	26.9

Spain	Budget balance (% of GDP)	Debt-to-GDP ratio (%)	Annual GDP growth (%)	Unemployment rate (%)
2007	1.9	36.1	4	8.5
2008	-4.5	40.2	2.5	9.6
2009	-11.2	53.9	-3.5	17.4
2010	-9.7	61.5	-1.4	20.1
2011	-9.4	69.3	0.5	21.3
2012	-10.6	84.2	-0.7	24.4
2013	N/A	N/A	-2	27.2

Portugal	Budget balance (% of GDP)	Debt-to-GDP ratio (%)	Annual GDP growth (%)	Unemployment rate (%)
2007	-3.1	68.3	2.6	8.4
2008	-3.6	71.7	0.9	7.6

2009	-10.2	83.7	-4.1	8.9
2010	-9.8	94	1.7	10.6
2011	-4.4	108.3	-0.4	12.4
2012	-6.4	123.6	-2.3	14.9
2013	N/A	N/A	-4	17.7

Italy	Budget balance (% of GDP)	Debt-to-GDP ratio (%)	Annual GDP growth (%)	Unemployment rate (%)
2007	-1.5	103.6	2.4	6
2008	-2.7	106.1	0.4	6.9
2009	-5.5	116.4	-6.5	7.4
2010	-4.5	119.3	1	8.8
2011	-3.8	120.8	0.8	8.2
2012	-3	127	-1.4	10.5
2013	N/A	N/A	-2.4	12.2

Cyprus	Budget balance (% of GDP)	Debt-to-GDP ratio (%)	Annual GDP growth (%)	Unemployment rate (%)
2007	3.5	58.8	5.2	4
2008	0.9	48.9	5	3.4
2009	-6.1	58.5	0.6	5.4
2010	-5.3	61.3	-0.5	6.4
2011	-6.3	71.1	1.7	7.5
2012	-6.3	85.8	-1.6	11.6
2013	N/A	N/A	-4.3	16.3

Ireland	Budget balance (% of GDP)	Debt-to-GDP ratio (%)	Annual GDP growth (%)	Unemployment rate (%)
2007	0.1	25	8.1	4.5
2008	-7.4	44.5	-0.4	6
2009	-13.9	64.8	-7.1	12.3
2010	-30.8	92.1	-2.9	13.7
2011	-13.4	106.4	-0.1	14.5
2012	-7.6	117.6	1.8	14.9
2013	N/A	N/A	-0.9	13.6

United Kingdom	Budget balance (% of GDP)	Debt-to-GDP ratio (%)	Annual GDP growth (%)	Unemployment rate (%)
2007	-2.7	44.5	2.6	5.4
2008	-5.1	52.3	2.7	5.4
2009	-11.2	73.9	-6.1	7.9
2010	-10.2	80	1.2	8
2011	-7.8	86.4	1.4	8
2012	-6.3	90.7	0.5	8.1
2013	N/A	N/A	0.3	7.8

Latvia	Budget balance (% of GDP)	Debt-to-GDP ratio (%)	Annual GDP growth (%)	Unemployment rate (%)
2007	-0.4	9	9	7.1
2008	-4.2	19.8	0.8	6.8
2009	-9.8	36.9	-17.8	14.3

2010	-8.1	44.4	-6.1	20.7
2011	-3.6	41.9	3.5	17.6
2012	-1.2	40.7	6.9	16.3
2013	N/A	N/A	3.6	12.8

Appendix B

I have reproduced a table from Theodoropoulou and Watt (2011, p.14), summarizing the extent/size of austerity programs in the European countries that had been decided on in 2010/2011. The original table also included the austerity package as percentage of GDP, but I decided not to include it, because the authors have not included all values for them.

	Austria	Bulgaria	Cyprus	Germany	Denmark	Spain	France	Greece	Hungary
Planned end-year	2014	2011	2013	2014	2013	2012	2014	2013	2010
Overall size of austerity package (bn of euro)	-13.6	-0.8	-0.3	-80	-3.3	-15.3	-83.2	-37.6	-9

	Ireland	Italy	Latvia	Luxembourg	Poland	Portugal	Sweden	United Kingdom
Planned end-year	2014-15	2012	2012	2014	2013	2013	2011	2015-16
Overall size of austerity package (bn of euro)	-22.3	-37	-2	-0.7	-0.2	-21.7	-1.4	-129

Index

"Agenda 2010" 76
Alesina, Alberto 66n43
Alitalia 23
Anglo-Irish Bank 37
Austerity
    Alternatives to 78-88
    Bailout of banks and 73-75
    Capital controls in 35
    Class effects of 65n42, 70, 81-82
    Cyprus 31-36
    Debt deflation in 35
    Disaster, social and economic 8
    Economic growth 35, impact of 75
    Eurozone and 70-73
    Export sector and 62-63
    Fallacy of 62-69
    GDP, correlation with 9
    Germany, promotion of 76-77
    Greece, in 7, purpose of 7
    Health care cuts in 36
    Income inequality and 66-67
    Investor confidence and 64-65
    Investor interests and 75-76
    Ireland, in 38-44, scholarly argument on 43-44
    Italy, in 24-30
    Latvia, in 55-61
    Origins of 70-75
    Portugal, in 16-22
    "Risk privatization" and 67
    Solutions to 78-88
    Spain, in 11-15
    Total package 8-9, 127-128
    United Kingdom 48-54;
    Treasury view of 48
    Wage share and 66-67
Austria 71-72, 84-85
    Competitiveness of 85
    Core country, as 71
    Creditor country, as 84
    Undervalued currency of 71-72
Banka Baltija 56
Bankia 10
Bank of Cyprus 33
Bank of England 45, 73
Bank of Greece 25
Bank of Japan 73
Banking crisis 10, 31, 37, 45, 56, 74
    Cyprus and 31
    Ireland and 37
    Latvia and 56
    Sovereign debt crisis and 74
    Spain and 10
    United Kingdom and 45
Basilicata 30
Beck, Ulrich 87-88
Bedroom tax 54
Belgium 81
Berlusconi, Silvio 24-25
Blyth, Mark 69n46
BNP Paribas 25
Brown, Gordon 45-48, 52
Calabria 30
California 85
Cameron, David 45, 48
Capital gains tax 16. 26, 65
    Italy and 26
    Portugal and 16
    Upper class people effect of 65
Catalonia 15
"Celtic Tiger" 37
Central Bank policy, low interest rates and bank liquidity 73
China 45, 63, 67
Class, social 65n42, 67, 70, 81-82, 89
Coelho, Pedro Passos 17-18
Collective bargaining, dismantling of 9, 12, 19
Conservative Party (UK) 45, 48-49, 52
Consumer confidence 6, 62, 65-67

Core countries (Eurozone) 71-72, 74, 76
Corporate tax 12, 35, 37, 40, 51
    Cyprus, increase in 35
    Ireland, low 37, maintenance of 40
    Spain, cuts in 12
    United Kingdom, cuts in 51
Cowen, Brian 39-40
Croke Park Agreement 40
Current account balance, comparison of 72
Current account deficit 10, 13-14, 27-28, 42, 52, 59, 72
    EU countries with 72
    Ireland and 42
    Italy and 27-28
    Latvia and 59
    Portugal and 20
    Spain and 10, 13-14
    United Kingdom and 52
Current account surplus 63, 72
    Difficulty with 63
    Germany and 72
    Netherlands and 72
Cyprus 6, 9, 31-36, 70, 89
    Austerity measures in 31-36
    Bank bailout in 32
    Capital controls in 33
    Depositor tax 33
    Education cuts in 36
    Economic growth 33-34
    Foundations of economy in 31
    Government bailout from IMF and EU in 33
    Greece, lending to 32
    Health care cuts in 36
    Labor strike and 32
    Privatization in 35
    Protests in 36
    Russian oligarchs and 31, 33
    Size of banking section in 31
    Tax haven, offshore as 31, loss of 33

Unemployment in 35
Darling, Alistair 46
Debt brake 67
Debt cancellation 78-80
Depardieu, Gerard 81
Depression (mental) 6, 15, 21, 89
    Portugal and 21
    Spain and 15
Devaluation, currency 23
    Austerity and 66
    Dismantling Eurozone and 82-84
    Iceland and 79
    Ireland, in 1980s 44
    Italy, traditional policy as 23
    Latvia, bet against 56, lack of 57, possible outcome of 59
    United Kingdom, option of 45, carrying out of 52
Devaluation, internal 44, 90
DnB ORD 56
Dombrovskis, Valdis 55, 57
Draghi, Mario 25
Economic growth -8, 13, 19, 23, 27, 41-42, 51, 55, 58
    Cyprus and 33-34
    Greece, outlook of 7-8
    Ireland and 41-42
    Italy and 23, 27
    Latvia and 55, 58
    Portugal and 19
    Spain and 13
    United Kingdom, recession and 51
EDP 17
Education cuts 6, 12, 21, 25, 29, 36, 43, 54, 61
    Cyprus and 36
    Ireland and 43
    Italy and 25, 29
    Latvia and 61
    Portugal and 21
    Spain and 12
    United Kingdom and 54

Emigration (see Immigrants)
Eurobank EFG 25
Euro bonds 87
Euro currency 7, 37, 57, 71
    Dismantling of 82-84
    Over- and undervaluation 71-72
Europe 6, 8-9, 11, 16, 37, 55, 56, 61, 62, 64, 66, 68, 70, 73, 76, 78, 80-85, 88-89, 90
    Alternative policies in 78
    Austerity package, size of 8-9, Germany and 76
    Bailout of banks in 73
    Capital inflows in Eastern 56
    Capital withdrawal from 80
    Euro currency, introduction of 70
    Debt of Southern 16
    Democratic and social 89
    Economic stagnation in 59
    Fiscal union in 85
    Hegemon in 87
    Inequality in 82
    Marshall Plan in 76, 84-86, impact on peripheral European countries 84
    Political mood in 90
    Social spending of 76
    Tax evasion in 81
    Wealthy creditors and 80-82
European Bank for Reconstruction and Development (ERBD) 56
European Central Bank 6, 73
    Banks, liquidity guarantee for 73
    Troika, as 7
European Commission 6, 7
    Troika, as 7
European Financial Stabilization Mechanism (EFSM) 74
European Marshall Plan 76, 84-85
European Stabilization Facility (ESFS) 74

European Union (EU)
    Alesina, Alberto, influence on policy 66
    Austerity policy, dictating of 83, 89
    Budget deficit in 81
    Cyprus, bailout of banks by 31, government bailout by 33; bailout guideline of 35, sense of betrayal of 36
    Fiscal treaty of 41, 76 (see Fiscal compact)
    Germany, paymaster of 90
    Greece, backstop debts by 68
    Ireland, bailout package of 39-40, bailout guidelines of 39, subsidy to 44
    Italy, Removal from crisis list by 27; bailout talks by 27
    Latvia, Yglesias, Matthew on 55, bailout of 56-57, bank influence on policy-making 58
    Loans by 75
    Parliamentary elections in 90
    Portugal, bailout package of 17; austerity guidelines of 19
    Spain, Rescue fund of 10; fiscal targets of 11-12
    Structural reforms, call for 9
    Tax evasion and loss of revenue 81
    United Kingdom, non-interference of 45
European Union Commissioner 19, 26, 32
Euroskeptic parties 90
Eurozone
    Bailout of banks within 74
    Core countries 74
    Crisis of 27, 45, 70, 75, German role in 75
    Currency peg in 71
    Dismantling of 78, 82-84, peripheral countries on 82-84,

Germany on 83, two-currency
unions 84
Fiscal union, lack of 73,
creation of 85-88, objections
to 86, historical experience of
86
Germany, beneficiary of 77
Greece debt in 75
Iceland and 79
Imbalance within 72-73
Latvia, accession to 55, 58;
desire to be part of 57-58
Peripheral countries 45, 64,
70, 74, 79, problems of
membership in 70; accession
to 70-71; speculator and
investor attacks against 74;
loans to 75, Swabian
housewife and 76; position on
dismantling of 83, Marshall
plan impact on 84;
competitiveness of 85
Unit labor costs in 76
Evora (Portugal) 21
Federal Reserve, US 73
Ferrari 26
Finland 56, 71, 84
    Bank investment in Latvia 56
    Core country, as 71
    Creditor country, as 84
Fiscal Compact 76
Fiscal target 11, 17, 50, 89
    Portugal and 17
    Spain and 11
    United Kingdom and 50
Fiscal union, EU 85-88
FMS Wertmanagement 25
France 25, 63-64, 71, 73, 81-82, 90
    Austerity policies 90
    Core country as 71
    Depardieu, Gerard and 81
    Greek debt to banks in 25
    Net importer, as 73
    Protests in 90

Trade deficit in 63
Wealth, rich people increase in
82
Galp Energia 17
Gaspar, Vitor 19
Germany 6, 9, 25, 62-64, 67, 71-73,
77-78, 83-88, 90
    "Agenda 2010" and
    competitiveness 76-77, 82
    Alternative for Germany
    (AfD) and 82
    Austerity policies, insistence
    on 75-76
    Bailout by 83
    Bank, foolish investments by
    67
    Current account surplus of 63
    Debt brake, proposal of 67
    Dismantling eurozone, views
    on 83, leaving currency union
    84
    Domestic demand, reluctance
    to raise 84
    Euro currency peg of 71,
    insistence on low inflation 71,
    export advantage of
    undervalued currency 71-72
    Export boom of 72
    Financier, as 9
    Fiscal union, role in 85-88
    Greek debt, holding of 25
    Merkel, Angela and 76
    Net exporter, as 73
    Paymaster, as 90
    "Unwilling hegemon", as 87-
    88
    Wage decline in 77
    Wealth, rich people increase in
    82
Goldman Sachs 25
Government bond interest rate 11, 16-
17, 23, 25, 38-39, 49, 65, 68, 70-71, 74,
79, 83
    Burden of hike of 74

Currency devaluation and 83
EU comparison of 70,
convergence of 70-71
Iceland and 79
Investor demand for high 64,
willingness to buy 65
Ireland and 38-39
Italy and 23, 25
Japan and 68
Portugal and 16-17
Spain and 11
United Kingdom and 45, 49
United States and 68
Government debt-to-GDP ratio 10-11, 16, 23-24, 27-28, 34-35, 38, 47-48, 52, 56-57, 68-69
    Austerity and 69
    Cyprus and 34-35
    Economic growth and 68
    Greece and 78
    Ireland and 38
    Italy and 23-24, 27-28
    Latvia and 56-57
    Portugal and 16
    Spain and 10-11
    United Kingdom and 47-48, 52
Greece 7-9, 16, 23, 25, 32, 55, 62-64, 68, 70-71, 75, 78, 83
    Austerity policies in 7, impact on consumption in 62-63
    Creditors of 25, loss of money (debt cancellation) in 75, 78
    Crisis impact on Portugal 16, Italy 23, Cyprus 32
    Currency devaluation, possible impacts in 83
    Dombrovskis, Valdis, advice to 55
    Economic growth outlook of 7-8
    EU-IMF loan for 7
    Euro currency peg in 71-72
    Fiscal union, impact of 85-88, problem with 87-88
    Government debt in 8, backstopping of debt in 68, bankroll consumption in 71
    Health care cuts in 8
    IMF demands on 9
    Infant mortality in 8
    Investor confidence in 64
    Labor market reform in 7
    Net importer, as 73
    Papademos, Lucas, Goldman Sachs and 25
    Poverty in 8
    Privatization and 9
    Productivity in 62
    Property tax in 7
    Protests in 22, 43
    Suicide rate increase in 8
    Tax evasion in 80
    Trade deficit in 63
    Wage cuts in 7
Grillo, Beppe 27
Health care cuts 6, 14-15, 21, 28-29, 36, 42-43, 54, 61
    Cyprus and 36
    Greece and 8
    Ireland and 42-43
    Italy and 28-29
    Latvia and 61
    Portugal and 21
    Spain and 14-15
    United Kingdom and 54
Health deterioration 66, 14-15, 21, 28-29, 36, 42-43, 54, 61
    Cyprus and 36
    Greece and 8
    Ireland and 42-43
    Italy and 28-29
    Latvia and 61
    Portugal and 21
    Spain and 14-15
    United Kingdom and 54
Herndon, Thomas 68
    Controversy with Reinhart and

Rogoff 68
Homeless rate increase 43, 53, 89
   Ireland and 43
   United Kingdom and 53
Howlin, Brendan 40
Iceland 56, 59-60, 78-80
   Bank investment in Latvia 56
   Comparison with Latvian economy 59-60
   Currency devaluation in 79
   Debt cancellation, as example 78-80
   Government bond purchase from 79
   Health improvement in 79
   Housing bubble in 78
Icelandic krona 78
IMF (International Monetary Fund) 6-8, 17, 19, 33, 39-40, 45, 50, 74 79, 83, 89
   Bailout funds provided by 74
   Cut in growth outlook 7-8
   Cyprus, bailout by and austerity advice by 33
   Greece, austerity advice by 7, "notable failure" of austerity 7, structural reform demand by 9
   Iceland, defiance of advice by 79
   Insistence on balanced budget by 89
   Ireland, bailout by and austerity advice by 39-40
   Loans and austerity 75
   Portugal bailout 17, austerity advice by 19
   Sovereignty of currency, impact on advice by 83
   United Kingdom, non-interference of 45, praise of fiscal consolidation efforts by 50
Immigrants 15, 30, 43, 58, 61, 91
   Blame on 91
   Ireland and emigration of 43
   Italy, and movement to northern part by 30
   Latvia and emigration of 58, 61
   Spain and exclusion from medical coverage of 15
Income tax 12, 16, 18, 31, 40, 46, 49-51, 58, 65, 81
   Cyprus, increase in 31, exemption for foreign workers 31
   Ireland, increase for low-income earners 40
   Latvia, increase in 58
   Portugal, increase in 16, 18
   Progressive, impact on upper class 65
   Spain, increase in 12
   Sweden, decrease in 81
   United Kingdom, increase in 46, cut in 49-51
Inequality 61, 67, 82, 90
Instituto de Estudios Fiscales 13
Interest rate (primary) 73-74
Internal devaluation 44-45, 57, 90
Investor
   Confidence of 6, 9, 48-49, 55, 64-65, 67
   Interests 75
   Willingness to purchase Icelandic bonds 79
Ireland 6, 9, 16, 23, 28, 37-44, 64, 70-71
   Austerity policies 38-44, social consequences of 42-43, scholarly arguments on 43-44
   Bailout of banks in 37
   "Celtic Tiger", as 37
   Corporate taxation in 37
   Crime increase in 43
   "Croke Park Agreement" and 40

Debt to GDP, comparison 28
Economic growth in 41-42
Education cuts in 43
Emigration of people from 43
EU fiscal treaty referendum 41
EU-IMF bailout to 39
Euro currency peg in 71
Government debt, increase in 73, budget balance in 37-38, debt to GDP ratio 38, bond interest rate 38
Health care cuts in 42-43
Housing bubble in 16, 37
Investor confidence in 64
Labor market reform ("structural reform") in 39
Private sector debt in 23, 71
Protests in 43
Suicide rate increase in 43
Unemployment in 37
Wage cuts in 42
Italy 6, 9, 23-30, 63-64, 70-73, 80
   Austerity measures in 24-30
   Bailout, lack of in 27
   Currency devaluation, impact on 83
   Current account balance in 27-28
   Deregulation in labor market in 26
   Economic growth in 23, 27
   Education cuts in 25, 29
   Eurozone membership of 70-72
   Food choices in 29-30
   Health care cuts in 28-29
   Investor confidence in 64
   Labor strike and 26
   Net importer, as 73
   Government debt 23, 71, 80, finance consumption 71, interest rate 23, budget deficit in 23
   Low productivity of 23
   North-South divide in 23
   Poverty in 30
   Privatization in 26
   Renzi, Matteo and 90
   Protests in 25 30
   "Salvia Italia" 26
   Southern Italy, impacts of austerity in 30
   Suicide rate increase in 30
   Trade deficit in 63
   Unemployment in 27
   Wage cuts in 32, lack of 27
   Wealth, rich people increase in 82
Japan 68
Kamprad, Ingvar 81
Kenny, Enda 40
Keynes, John Maynard 48
Keynesian stimulus 85
King, Mervyn 45
Labor market reform 6, 12, 19, 26, 39
   Greece and 7
   Ireland and 39
   Italy and 26
   Portugal and 19
   Spain and 12
Labor strike 16, 22, 25, 32, 40
   Cyprus and 32
   Ireland, Croke Park agreement and abstention from 40
   Italy and 25
   Portugal and 16, 22
Labour Party (UK) 45, 48
Lagarde, Christine 80
Laiki bank 33
Latvia 6, 9, 33, 55-61, 70, 89
   Austerity measures in 57-58, social consequences of 60-61
   Bank crisis (1990s) in 55-56
   Economic growth, rebound in 55, GDP growth 58
   Education cuts in 61
   Emigration of 58

Eurozone accession of 57-58, 70
Export sector in 59
Foreign capital inflow, dependence on 56-57
Health care cuts in 61
Household consumption, decline of 59
Poverty in 60-61
Protests in 61
Role model for other EU countries 55
Russian oligarch money in 33
Suicide rate increase in 61
Transportation cuts in 61
Unemployment in 58
Wage cuts in 59

Letta, Enrico 27
Liberal Democrats (UK) 48
Löfven, Stefan 90
Madrid 15
Merkel, Angela 67, 76
Minimum wage 7, 9, 13, 19, 40, 46-47
   Greece, cuts 7, IMF demand for cuts 9
   Ireland, cuts 40
   Portugal, freezing of 19
   Spain, Central bank demand for cuts 13
   United Kingdom, increase 46-47
Mississippi 85
Monti, Mario 25-27
Mordovia (Russia) 81
National debt 6-9, 10-11, 16, 23-24, 27, 38-39, 46-47, 52, 62, 64-67, 71, 73-75, 78-81, 83, 86-89
   Austerity measures' impact on 64-67, hope to reduce 74-75
   Bank bailout and 73
   Bankrolling consumption and 71
   Cancellation of 78-80
   Currency inflation, impact on 83
   Cyprus, in 34-35
   Economic growth and 62, impacted by 67-69
   Eurozone entry and sustainability of 71
   Fiscal union and assumption of common 86-88
   Greece, in 7-8
   Investor confidence and 64, interest and 75
   Ireland, in 38-39
   Italy, in 23-24, 27
   Latvia, in 56-57
   Marx, Karl, view on 80
   Portugal, in 16
   Spain, in 10-11
   Taxing the rich and 81
   United Kingdom, in 46-47, 52
National Health Service 54
National Institute for Economic and Social Research 50
Netherlands 71-73, 79, 84
   Core country, as 71
   Creditor country, as 84
   Creditor of Iceland, as 79
   Export boom in 72
   Net exporter, as 73
New York 85
Nordea 56
Norvik 56
Norway 56
   Bank investment in Latvia by 56
Ortega, Amancio 82
Osborne, George 48-51
Papaconstantinou, George 80
Papademos, Lucas 25
Parex Bank 56
Parliamentary elections, EU 90
Pensions, cuts 7, 12-13, 18, 24-26, 31-32, 39, 46-47, 50-51, 75, 82, 89
   Bank bailouts and 75, 82
   Cyprus and 31-32, penalty on

early retirement 31
Greece and 7, retirement age increase 7
Ireland and 39
Italy and 24, 26, retirement age increase 25-26
Portugal, retirement age increase 18
Spain and 13, retirement age increase 12
United Kingdom and 47,50-51, increase in pensions 46, retirement age increase 50
Peripheral countries 45, 64, 70, 74, 79
    Accession to 70-71
    Competitiveness of 85
    Loans to 75
    Marshall plan impact on 84
    Position on dismantling of Eurozone by 83
    Problems of eurozone membership in 70
    Speculator and investor attacks against 74
    Swabian housewife and 76
Piraeus Bank 25
Portugal 6, 9, 16-22, 23, 27, 62, 64, 70-73
    Aging population and 16
    Austerity policies of 16-22
    Economic growth in 19
    Education cuts in 21
    Government deficit of 16, debt of 23, temporary decline in 17, support of consumption 71
    Health care cuts in 21
    Investor confidence in 64
    Labor market reform in 19
    Labor strike in 16
    Low growth of 16
    Low productivity of 16, 23
    Net importer, as 73
    Overvaluing of currency of 72
    Privatization in 17-18
    Protests in 21-22
    Trade balance, negative in 62
    Unemployment in 19-20
    Wage cuts in 16-17, 20
Portugal Telecom 17
Poverty 6, 8, 15, 30, 60-61
    Greece and 8
    Italy and 30
    Latvia and 60-61
    Spain and 15
Privatization 6, 9, 17-18, 26,35, 67
    Cyprus and 35
    Greece and 9
    Italy and 26
    Portugal and 17-18
    Risk 67
    Spain and 12
Property bubble 10, 37, 67, 78
    German investment and 67
    Iceland and 78
    Ireland and 37
    Spain and 10
Property tax, increase
    Cyprus and 32, 35
    Greece and 7
    Ireland and 40-41
Protests 6, 15, 21-22, 25, 30, 36, 43, 54, 61, 90
    Cyprus and 36
    France and 90
    Greece and 22, 43
    Ireland and 43
    Italy and 25, 30
    Latvia and 61
    Portugal and 21-22
    Spain and 15
    United Kingdom and 54
Public-sector workers 6-7, 16, 18, 24, 35, 39-40, 44, 13, 48-52, 58
    Layoff, Greece 7, Cyprus 35, Ireland 40, Portugal 18, United Kingdom 48-50
    Pay cuts, Greece 7, Spain 11, Portugal 16, Italy 24, Cyprus

35, Ireland 39-40, United
Kingdom and 49, 51, Latvia
58
Pay increase, Ireland 44,
United Kingdom 46, 52
Work increase, Portugal 18,
Ireland 40
Putin, Vladimir 33
Retirement age (see pensions)
Rajoy, Mariano 11
Rehn, Oli 19, 32
Renzi, Matteo 90
Riga Commerce Bank 56
"Risk privatization" and 67
Russia 31, 33
    Depardieu, Gerard, and
    citizenship in 81
    Financial crisis impact on
    Latvia 56
    Oligarch money in Cyprus 31,
    33, transfer to Latvia 33
Sales tax, increase
    Cyprus and 35
    Non-wealthy people effects of
    82
    Portugal and 16, 18
    Spain and 12
Salvia Italia 26
Sardinia 28
SEB 56
Sicily 28
Socrates, Jose 16
Soviet Union 55
Spain 6, 9, 10-15, 16, 20, 23, 27-28, 37, 43, 62-64, 70-73, 80, 82, 89
    Ortega, Amancio and 82
    Austerity measures in 11-15,
    impact on economy in 13-14,
    failure in 89
    Budget balance in 10
    Central bank and 13
    Corporate tax cuts in 12
    Economic growth in 13
    Education cuts in 12

Export competitiveness and 20
Euro currency crisis and 70-71
EU bailout for 10
Government bailout of banks
in 10, debt in 10, financial
market punishment of 11
Health care cuts in 14-15
Investor confidence in 64
Labor market reform in 12
Labor strike and 12
Net importer, as 73
Overvaluing of currency of 72
Poverty in 15
Private sector debt in 23
Privatization in 12
Property bubble in 10
Protests in 15
Social problems in 14-15
Suicide rate increase in 15
Trade balance, negative in 62-63
Unemployment in 13
Wage cuts in 11, 13, 27
Stimulus program 6, 11, 27, 46, 84-85
    EU-wide 84-85
    Italy 27
    Spain 11
    United Kingdom 46
Suicide rate, increase of 6, 8, 15, 30, 61 89
    Greece and 8
    Ireland and 43
    Italy and 30
    Spain and 15
    Latvia and 61
Swedbank 56
Sweden 56, 81, 90
    Bank investment in Latvia 56
    Kamprad, Ingvar and 81
    Löfven, Stefan and 90
Switzerland 81-82
    Kamprad, Ingvar and 81
    Wealth, rich people increase in
    82

Tax evasion 80-81
Tennessee 85
Treasury view 48
Troika 6-7
Unemployment 6, 13, 19-20, 27, 35, 37, 52, 58
    Cyprus and 35
    Greece and 7, youth 7
    Ireland and 37
    Italy and 27, youth 28
    Latvia and 58
    Portugal and 19-20
    Spain and 13, youth 13
    United Kingdom and 52
United Kingdom 6, 9, 42, 45-54, 58-59, 63, 70, 79, 89
    Austerity policies in , 49-54, voluntary in 45, 89, social consequences of 53-54
    Bank bailout in 45
    Bedroom tax in 54
    Comparison of GDP with Latvia 59
    Conservative rule, beginning of 48
    Corporation cash-holding in 49
    Creditor of Iceland, as 79
    Currency devaluation in 52
    Economic recession in 51
    Education cuts in 54
    Eurozone and 70
    Exports from Ireland into 42
    Government borrowing costs in 45, debt to GDP ratio 52, budget deficit in 52
    Health care cuts in 54
    Iceland lawsuit by 79
    Protests in 54
    Stimulus program in 46-47
    Trade deficits of 63
    "Treasury view" in 48
    Unemployment in 52
    Wage cuts in 52-53, 58
United States 8, 42
    Comparison in economic performance with Latvia 59
    Economic growth, anticipated in 8
    Fiscal union in 85
    Exports from Ireland to 42
Vaxevanis, Kostas 81
Vienna 57
Wage cuts 6, 16-17, 20, 32, 40, 58-59, 66, 75, 83, 90
    Bank bailout and 75
    Consumer confidence and 66
    Dismantling of Eurozone and 83
    Germany and 77
    Greece and 7
    Internal devaluation and 90
    Ireland and 42, minimum wage cuts 40
    Italy, lack of 27, implementation of 32
    Latvia and 58-59
    Portugal and 16-17, 20
    Problem with 62
    Spain and 11, 13, 27
    United Kingdom and 52-53, 58
Wage share, declining 67
Wealth Tax 80-82
Welfare cuts 6, 26, 41, 50, 52, 54
    Ireland and 41
    Italy and 26
    United Kingdom and 50, 52, 54
Welfare state 90
Work week, lengthening of 40, 18
    Ireland and 40
    Portugal and 18
Yglesias, Matthew 55
Zapatero, Jose Luis Rodriguez 11

About the Author:

L.(Liam Ching) Larry Liu is an undergraduate in the University of Pennsylvania, studying sociology and economic policy, and currently resides in Philadelphia. His research interests include the political economy of Europe, comparative labor market institutions, economic history of developed countries, political sociology and class relations in East and Southeast Asia, technological effects on employment, inequality and social stratification, among others.

A few examples of his work include
"Anti-Government Protests in Thailand: A Political Sociology of Elite and Class Conflict." *Penn Asian Review* 4 (2014): 18-23.
"Hakka Chinese Political Leadership in East and Southeast Asia, and South America." (unpublished) September 2014.
"Salesworkers in the Twenty-First Century: The Effects of Technological Change on Retail and Financial Service Employment." Independent Study, University of Pennsylvania, Department of Sociology. April 2014.
"Codetermination: Trade Union Power in Germany and the US." Sociology of Law Course, University of Pennsylvania, Department of Sociology. February 2014.

He can be reached by e-mail for critiques and comments: liam.ching.liu@gmail.com

www.ingramcontent.com/pod-product-compliance
Lightning Source LLC
Chambersburg PA
CBHW051713170526
45167CB00002B/644